This book is to be returned on or before

Groupwork
With Children
of Battered
Women

Interpersonal Violence: The Practice Series

Jon R. Conte, Series Editor

Interpersonal Violence: The Practice Series is devoted to mental health, social service, and allied professionals who confront daily the problem of interpersonal violence. It is hoped that the knowledge, professional experience, and high standards of practice offered by the authors of these volumes may lead to the end of interpersonal violence.

In this series...

Groupwork
With Children
of Battered
Women

A Practitioner's Guide

Einat Peled
Diane Davis

Interpersonal Violence:
The Practice Series

SAGE Publications
International Educational and Professional Publisher
Thousand Oaks London New Delhi

Copyright © 1995 by Sage Publications, Inc.

For information address:

 SAGE Publications, Inc.
2455 Teller Road
Thousand Oaks, California 91320

SAGE Publications Ltd.
6 Bonhill Street
London EC2A 4PU
United Kingdom

SAGE Publications India Pvt. Ltd.
M-32 Market
Greater Kailash I
New Delhi 110 048 India

Printed in the United States of America

Library of Congress Cataloging-in-Publication Data

Peled, Einat.
    Groupwork with children of battered women: a practitioner's
manual / authors, Einat Peled, Diane Davis.
        p.   cm.—(Interpersonal violence: the practice series; v. 10)
    Includes bibliographical references and index.
    ISBN 0-8039-5514-6.—ISBN 0-8039-5515-4 (pbk.)
    1. Children of abused wives—Mental health services. 2. Group
psychotherapy for children. 3. Children of abused wives—Mental
health. I. Davis, Diane, 1948- . II. Title. III. Series:
Interpersonal violence; v. 10.
RJ507.F53P45   1995
618.92'89152—dc20   94-34630

95 96 97 98 99 10 9 8 7 6 5 4 3 2 1

Sage Production Editor: Diana E. Axelsen

Contents

Acknowledgments

This manual is based on years of education and counseling provided by the Domestic Abuse Project (DAP) of Minneapolis to more than 750 children.

DAP was established in 1979 to expand the ways social programs intervened to stop woman abuse. It provides four complementary programs: therapy, community intervention, evaluation and research, and training (for a full description of DAP's philosophy and programs, see Brygger & Edleson, 1987).

The therapy program offers educational/process groups for men, women, and children. The community intervention program works with social and legal services to ensure a consistent and unified response to the problem of domestic violence. Individual legal advocacy on specific cases is also made available to many victims. The evaluation and research program investigates, develops, and evaluates treatment modalities that are most effective in ending abuse. The training program at DAP includes clinical practicums for students and professionals within the agency and a variety of workshops and seminars designed to increase the skills of participants in domestic violence intervention and treatment.

DAP may be reached at:

> Domestic Abuse Project (DAP)
> 204 West Franklin Avenue
> Minneapolis, MN 55404
> Tel. (612) 874-7063
> Fax. (612) 874-8445

Evaluation of DAP's children's program and this manual have been made possible through the support of a grant from the Emma B. Howe Foundation of Minneapolis. We are grateful to the administrative and therapy staff at the Domestic Abuse Project and to interns at DAP's children's program for supporting the preparation of this manual. We owe special thanks to Jeffrey Edleson, who headed the children's program evaluation project and gave us invaluable editorial assistance. Thanks also to Elaine Amond, Joan Bilinkoff, Greg Bowden, Dave Dipman, Mary Linnihan, Shannon Schmidt, and Harry Schusser, who generously shared their practice wisdom and reviewed earlier drafts of this manual. Special thanks are in order to Lorraine Hecht, who conducted many evaluation interviews, and to Susan Raskin, who helped with library research for this manual.

Comments and suggestions by many children's advocates and counselors from all over the United States who sent us feedback on the first draft of this manual were helpful and greatly appreciated. Good advice and editorial comments were offered by Jon Conte, the Series Editor. We thank Jon for his persistence and patience in helping us see the taken-for-granted and in making it explicit. We also acknowledge the ongoing support and encouragement of C. Terry Hendrix, Sage's Interpersonal Violence Editor.

Last, but not least, we thank the children, mothers, and fathers who participated in DAP's groups and in the research and who taught us so much of what we know. It is to them we dedicate this book.

Introduction

This manual is designed specifically for practitioners who currently facilitate or would like to start a group program for 4- to 12-year-old children of battered women. It provides group leaders with a detailed description and discussion of the group program units, as well as with the knowledge base required for successful operation of such a program.

Our manual is based on the accumulated experience of the childrens program at the Domestic Abuse Project (DAP) of Minneapolis and on the results of a qualitative evaluation of DAP's program conducted in the years 1989 to 1991 (see Peled & Edleson, 1992; also see Chap. 1 for evaluation results).

The childrens program and this manual are guided by the theoretical and philosophical preassumptions adopted by DAP (see Box I.1).

The program information presented in this manual is based on work and research with children of mostly white, heterosexual, battered women. Hence it may not be adapted fully to the needs of children of battered women of color or of gay and lesbian victims /survivors. However, we consider sensitivity to culture and sexual orientation to be a crucial element in effective and successful inter-

---

Box I.1: DAP's Guiding Presumptions

- Abuse is a result of unequal power balance in intimate heterosexual, gay, and lesbian relationships. Institutions support and encourage domestic abuse through policy and practice.
- Battering is a learned behavior and as such can be unlearned and replaced with more productive ways of interacting.
- Abusers use violence to exert control, to relieve built-up tension, to take revenge, and/or to keep people away. Victims/survivors stay in the relationship for a variety of reasons, including fear, lack of alternatives, family and societal pressure, and economic and emotional dependency. They do not stay because they want or deserve to be abused. Domestic abuse is never the victim's/survivor's or the child's fault.
- Violence itself is not caused by a poor intimate relationship, job frustration, sexual problems, or child-rearing problems, although these factors are most likely present and will cause stress.
- Alcohol and other drugs are not the cause of battering, and chemical dependency issues must be dealt with separately.
- The primary goal of treatment for abusers is to stop the violent behavior, not to save the relationship. For the victims/survivors, it is to increase their ability to protect themselves; for the children, it is to heal from the effects of violence and to learn new conflict resolution skills.
- New social support systems must be developed for men and women that do not reinforce abuse, but that encourage free expression of emotion and break down social isolation and complete emotional reliance on the partner.
- Abuse hurts all individuals in the family setting, and intervention should be available to all members of the family.
- Relationship counseling can be effective only after the abuser has taken responsibility for and learned to control the violent behavior and the victim/survivor has relinquished responsibility for the violence and is no longer afraid of retaliation by the abuser.

---

vention with child witnesses of domestic violence and hope this manual can benefit children from various populations.

The majority of this manual is devoted to a detailed description of the group program. Briefly, prior to entering the group, each child is assessed for a history of physical abuse and neglect, sexual abuse, and for the emotional impact of witnessing abuse. Each child and at least one parent, usually the mother, participate in an assessment process through individual and joint interviews with a group leader. A child usually will enter a group that is led by a male-female team of therapists who often are also working with the children's parents in adult groups. Groups meet once each week over a 10-week period for an hour-long session.

Concurrent educational groups are available to the parents to enhance their parenting skills. In addition, a family session ordinarily is conducted after the children's last group meeting. Family sessions are designed to review the material covered in children's groups and for the parents to receive recommendations on additional services that might be helpful for the individual child, as well as for the family.

Chapter 1 reviews current knowledge about the impact on children of witnessing violence of battered women and about group intervention with these children. Chapter 2 introduces the goals and subgoals on which the program is based. Chapter 3 delineates the intake process for the group, explains the use of different intake forms (see Appendix A), and provides group leaders with criteria for group participation and outside referral of children who are assessed for the group. The orientation, group sessions, and family session are described and discussed in detail in Chapter 4. A supplement to this chapter, a sample of the session-specific Desired Outcomes Evaluation Form, is given in Appendix B. Finally, Chapter 5 provides group leaders with major themes and facilitating tips for a parenting group that may be conducted in conjunction with the children's group.

1

Current Knowledge About Children of Battered Women

The program described in this manual draws on the extensive experience of DAP staff in working directly with child witnesses and their parents and on our recent qualitative evaluation of this program. It also draws on (a) studies of the effects that witnessing woman abuse has on children and (b) literature regarding other programs for children of battered women. This chapter reviews existing knowledge about children of battered women, emphasizing research findings in this domain.

❑ Witnessing Violence

The world in which we raise our children is extremely violent. Millions of children are victims of child physical and sexual abuse every year (Dubowitz, 1986; Straus & Gelles, 1986) or witness the abuse of their siblings. Many more children are frequent witnesses of media violence; they watch it, hear it, read about it, and play with it. Violence is a major theme of television shows, movies, newscasts, music, sports, literature, and children's toys (Miedzian, 1991); it is rampant on many of the streets of this country (Garbarino, Dubrow, Kostelny, & Pardo, 1992; Kotlowitz, 1991); and it is a constant presence in families in which the mother is being abused. Although the focus of this manual is on child witnesses of woman battering, it is important to remember that these children often also experience and witness other forms of violence.

The phenomenon of children witnessing violence directed at their mothers, as described by professionals or as studied by researchers, encompasses a wide range of experiences:

> Children may observe this violence directly by seeing their father (or another intimate partner of their mother) threaten or hit their mother. They may overhear this behavior from another part of the residence, such as their own bedroom. Children may be exposed to the results of this violence without hearing or seeing the commission of any aggressive act. Less commonly, children may be exposed to isolated incidents of violence. (Jaffe, Wolfe, & Wilson, 1990, p. 17)

It is estimated that between 3.3 million (Carlson, 1984) and 10 million (Straus, 1991) children in the United States are yearly at risk of witnessing woman battering. This high number is probably not a recent development. Evidence suggests that children have been witnessing their mothers being abused throughout history (e.g., Edleson, 1991; Gordon, 1988; Pleck, 1987), but their predicament started to attract professional and public attention only in the late 1970s. The professional interest in children of battered women seemed to have been contingent on the relatively recent construction of marital violence into a social problem (Loseke, 1987; Straus, Gelles, & Steinmetz, 1980) and to draw on existing public and professional awareness of the problem of child abuse in general (Nelson, 1984) and child psychological abuse in particular (Brassard, Germain, & Hart, 1983; Garbarino, Guttmann, & Seeley, 1986).

❏ Psychological Maltreatment

Child witnessing of domestic violence can be seen as psychological abuse of the child, defined by Garbarino and his colleagues (1986) as a "concrete attack by an adult on a child's development of self and social competence, a *pattern* of psychically destructive behavior" (p. 8).

> *Child witnessing of domestic violence can be seen as psychological abuse of the child.*

The psychological maltreatment of child witnesses can take three forms: (a) terrorizing, (b) living in dangerous environments, and (c) exposure to limiting and negative role models. The child witness is terrorized when the adult perpetrator of violence verbally assaults the child, creates a climate of fear, bullies and frightens the child, and makes the child believe that the world is capricious and hostile (Garbarino et al., 1986). Brassard et al. (1983) suggest that a child in a situation of high crime and violence or severe family instability is maltreated by having to live in a dangerous and unstable environment. Finally, the child witness who is provided models of narrow, rigid, self-destructive, violent, and/or antisocial behaviors by the perpetrator of violence is emotionally abused by being influenced by negative and limiting role models (Brassard et al., 1983).

In the light of these definitions, we suggest that the perpetrator of violence is abusing not only the woman but also the children who witness such violence. Furthermore, it provides us with some insight into the processes through which the witnessed violence affects the child.

❏ Children in Battered Women's Shelters

Advocates, clinicians, and researchers who worked with and studied battered women were the first to report on children of battered women (e.g., Dobash & Dobash, 1979; Hilberman & Munson, 1977-1978; Martin, 1976; Stacy & Shupe, 1983; Walker, 1979). These professionals, faced with battered women's concerns for their children

---

Box 1.1: Shelter Conditions Affecting Children

- Recent crisis following the witnessing of violence at home
- Disruption of normal coping patterns and support systems after separation from father, friends, school, home, and so forth
- Rapid adjustment to a new living situation, including new living quarters, unfamiliar people, new school, and new rules
- Difficult living conditions, including lack of privacy and high emotional intensity displayed by other residents
- Emotional or physical unavailability of mother because of her own emotional turmoil and practical demands imposed by the need to rearrange family life

---

and the difficulties experienced by the children themselves, described emotional and physical difficulties experienced by children residing in shelters for battered women (e.g., Elbow, 1982; Hilberman & Munson, 1977-1978; Layzer, Goodson, & Delange, 1986; Levine, 1975; Moore, 1975).

Attention has been given to the health problems from which children in shelters suffer (Kerouac, Taggart, Lescop, & Fortin, 1986; Layzer et al., 1986); acute feelings of loss, anger, fear, sadness, confusion, and guilt; and a variety of adjustment problems (Alessi & Hearn, 1984; Carlson, 1984; Cassady, Allen, Lyon, & McGeehan, 1987; Jaffe et al., 1990; Layzer et al., 1986). These various problems were seen as a result of the conditions listed in Box 1.1.

Unfortunately, on the one hand, no systematic research has been done on the adjustment of children to shelter life, and so we know little about the interaction between the above five conditions and the different patterns of children's adjustment problems. However, several studies have documented the effects of witnessing violence on children's behavior while taking into consideration other personal and situational mediating variables (e.g., Davis & Carlson, 1987; Hughes, 1988; Rosenbaum & O'Leary, 1981; Wolfe, Jaffe, Wilson, & Zak, 1988).

❑ The Effects on Children of Witnessing Woman Battering

At least 18 studies so far have measured the effects of witnessing violence on children's behavioral problems and adjustment. Overall, these studies found children of battered women to have significantly more adjustment problems than comparison groups of children from nonviolent homes (Fantuzzo et al., 1991; Holden & Ritchie, 1991; Hughes, Parkinson, & Vargo, 1989; Hughes, Vargo, Ito, & Skinner, 1991; Jaffe, Wolfe, Wilson, & Zak, 1986a; Jouriles, Murphy, & O'Leary, 1989; Wolfe, Jaffe, Wilson, & Zak, 1985; Wolfe et al., 1988).

Studies found child witnesses to have more overall externalizing problem behavior (Jaffe, Wolfe, Wilson, & Zak, 1986b), more overall internalizing problem behavior (Christopherpoulos et al., 1987), and less social competence (Wolfe, Zak, Wilson, & Jaffe, 1986).

Children of battered women were also found to show more anxiety (Forsstrom-Cohn & Rosenbaum, 1985; Hughes, 1988), more aggression (Westra & Martin, 1981), more temperamental problems (Holden & Ritchie, 1991), more depression (Christopherpoulos et al., 1987), less empathy (Hinchey & Gavelek, 1982), less self-esteem (Hughes, 1988), and lower verbal, cognitive, and motor abilities (Westra & Martin, 1981) than children who did not witness violence at home. These adjustment problems were related to several factors other than the witnessing of violence.

FACTORS MEDIATING THE INFLUENCE
OF WITNESSING VIOLENCE

Research suggested that exposure to woman battering negatively affects the behavior and emotional well-being of children. However, the relationship between the violence and its effects on the children is multidimensional and complex. The effects of violence on witnessing children are mediated by many personal and situational factors. These factors, such as age, gender, and living circumstances, may vary among children and mediate the influence of the witnessed

Many personal and situational factors mediate the effects of violence on witnessing children.

violence in different ways. Mediating factors studied by researchers of child witnesses are severity of violence witnessed, child abuse, gender of child, age of child, race of child, maternal stress, child-rearing practices, time of exposure to violence, and impact of shelter residence. Each of these factors is discussed below.

Severity of Violence Witnessed. Although the adverse effects of marital conflict and divorce on children are well documented (e.g., Gyrch & Fincham, 1990; Wallerstein & Kelly, 1980), children from maritally violent families seem to have more behavioral problems than children from maritally discordant families (Forsstrom-Cohn & Rosenbaum, 1985; Jouriles et al., 1989). For example, Fantuzzo and his colleagues (1991) found that children who were exposed to both physical and verbal violence exhibited more behavioral problems than children who witnessed only verbal abuse.

Child Abuse. It is estimated that 30% to 40% of all children of battered women are abused themselves (Hotaling & Straus, 1989). Estimates based on shelter populations are even higher. Layzer and her colleagues (1986) studied residents of five shelters for battered women in different states and found that 70% of the children were victims of abuse or neglect.

Child witnesses of woman battering who were also physically or sexually abused were found to have more behavioral problems than nonabused child witnesses (Davis & Carlson, 1987; Fantuzzo et al., 1991; Hughes, 1988; Hughes et al., 1989; Jaffe et al., 1986b; Jouriles et al., 1989; Pfouts, Schopler, & Hanley, 1981).

Gender. Although findings regarding the effect of child abuse were clear, studies of the influence of gender on behavioral problems in child witnesses provided mixed results. Furthermore, gender differences seem to be tied to the age of the child.

In preschool children, girls showed less empathy (Hinchey & Gavelek, 1982) and more anxiety (Hughes & Barad, 1983) than boys. Boys, however, had more externalizing and internalizing problem behavior (Stagg, Wills, & Howell, 1989) and more aggression, depression, and somatic symptoms (Davis & Carlson, 1987).

Among school-age children, girls exhibited more overall behavioral problems, aggression (Christopherpoulos et al., 1987; Davis & Carlson, 1987), and internalizing problems (Holden & Ritchie, 1991) than boys. However, in other studies, school-age boys had more behavioral problems in general and aggression in particular (Jaffe et al., 1986b; Jouriles et al., 1989; Westra & Martin, 1981; Wolfe et al., 1985).

Adolescent males exposed to marital violence were more likely to run away from home and to report suicidal thoughts than adolescent females (Carlson, 1990). However, college-age women from maritally violent homes reported more depression than males with a similar background (Forsstrom-Cohn & Rosenbaum, 1985).

Age. The results of studies measuring age differences among child witnesses are also somewhat contradictory. School-age children were found to have more behavioral problems than preschool children (Davis & Carlson, 1987; Holden & Ritchie, 1991; Hughes et al., 1989). In another study, however, preschool children were found to have more behavioral problems than school-age children (Hughes, 1988).

Race. Only two studies measured race as a possible mediating variable for the effects of witnessed violence on the child. These studies found white children to have more behavioral problems and less motor ability than nonwhite children (Stagg et al., 1989; Westra & Martin, 1981).

Maternal Stress and Child-Rearing Practices. Several studies measured the influence of situational family factors on the effects of witnessing violence. Some found maternal stress (a combination of maternal health, negative life events, and family disadvantage) and reported father's irritability to be related to behavioral problems of child witnesses (Holden & Ritchie, 1991; Wolfe et al., 1985; Wolfe et al., 1986; Wolfe et al., 1988).

Holden and Ritchie (1991) did not find differences in parenting behaviors of battered and nonbattered women. However, they did find child-rearing to be perceived as more stressful by battered women than by nonbattered women. Possibly related to this were three other findings regarding fathers' involvement, inconsistency in parenting, and conflict. First, fathers' involvement with children, as reported by mothers, was lower for violent men than for nonviolent men, and the former were reported to be less physically affectionate and to use more physical punishment. Second, battered women reported more inconsistency in parenting than nonbattered women. This was manifested through the use of discipline methods different from the fathers' and alteration of child-rearing behaviors in the presence of the father. Third, more conflict was observed in mother-child interactions of battered women than in those of nonbattered women.

Time of Exposure to Violence and Shelter Residence. Wolfe and his colleagues (1986) found that current residents of a shelter who were exposed to woman battering within 6 weeks preceding the interview had more social competence problems than former residents who were not exposed to violence for the past 6 months. In another study (Fantuzzo et al., 1991), children residing in a shelter experienced higher levels of internalizing problem behavior and lower levels of social competency and perceived maternal acceptance than children of battered women living at home.

Summary. There seems to be some agreement among studies that additional experiences with violence compound the adverse effects of witnessing on the children. Children who were both witnesses of violence and abused themselves were at a greater risk for developing problem behavior than children who were witnesses of violence but were not abused. Furthermore, children who witnessed both verbal and physical violence suffered from more behavioral problems than children who witnessed only verbal abuse.

Additional experiences with violence compound the adverse effects of witnessing violence.

Two situational variables also seemed to be clearly related to the extent of the effect of violence on children. First, maternal stress and paternal irritability, both at least partially related to the violence, increased the negative effects of witnessing violence on the child.

Second, a shelter stay, also associated with proximity to the time of witnessing violence, was related to higher levels of problem behavior in children. These research results corroborated earlier reports of shelter workers discussed above regarding the adverse effects of shelter conditions and mother's unavailability on children's emotions and behavior.

The picture regarding gender, age, and race differences, however, is unclear. Although these factors seemed to mediate the influence of violence on the children, clear patterns of influence are hard to trace among the different and often contrasting findings. Gyrch and Fincham (1990), in a review of the literature on the impact of marital conflict on children's adjustment, similarly concluded that interparental conflict is associated with adjustment problems in both boys and girls and that age appears to be unrelated to the incidence or severity of behavioral problems.

CRITIQUE OF RESEARCH ON CHILD WITNESSES OF DOMESTIC VIOLENCE

An integration of research findings on child witnesses of domestic violence should be approached with caution and regarded as tentative, in the light of the following research shortcomings:

Sample. The sample of reviewed studies differed greatly in many important characteristics—most notably size, age, and income—and these differences were likely to influence the results. In most studies, race, mental health, shelter residency, and abuse status of the subjects were not controlled for or even registered. However, these factors may mediate the influence of violence on witnessing children.

Measures. The multiplicity of measures used for problem behaviors rendered the comparison and integration of their results difficult, if not impossible. Furthermore, satisfactory validity and reliability procedures were not reported for some of the measures used. Although a relatively large number of studies used the well-established Child Behavior Checklist (Achenbach & Edelbrock, 1983) and Behavior Problem Checklist (Quay, 1977), these measures were used with noncomparable samples and in combination with a variety of other measures.

About half of the reviewed studies used mothers' reports on the original version of the Conflict Tactics Scale (CTS) (Straus, 1979) as a measure for marital violence. Only a few studies specifically measured the child's direct witnessing of violence. As a result, most studies did not distinguish between a child's direct witnessing of violence and a child's residence with maritally violent parents. The two experiences and their consequences for the child, however, may be dramatically different. Moreover, the frequency, severity, and intent of the violence received almost no attention.

Sources of Information. Child witnesses of violence constituted the target group in all studies, but only in about half of the studies were they, at least partially, the source of information. The majority of studies used mothers as the chief source of information about their children's problem behavior and witnessed violence. The results, therefore, should be seen as primarily reflecting the mother's point of view on these conditions.

The existing literature on child witnesses of domestic violence is primarily pathology-oriented. As such, it provides documentation of the problems experienced by these children but adds little to our knowledge of the strengths of the children or to our understanding of the ways they manage their difficult life situations and of the role of the violence in their lives.

A review of the empirical literature suggests several implications for practitioners working with child witnesses of domestic violence. As noted above, the approach used by the reviewed studies focuses professional attention on psychopathologies and developmental impairments of the witnessing children, as well as on parenting inadequacies. This approach may contribute to the revictimization of both battered women and their children. The need is for an alternative perspective that will emphasize children's strengths and resiliency and regard child witnesses of violence as secondary victims of the abuser and the current power imbalances in the social structure. Such definitions, though not precluding immediate individual intervention with child witnesses and their parents, may prevent further victimization of the victim/survivor and her children by focusing the responsibility for the problem on the abuser and the social structure. It also may extend intervention efforts to include the facilitation and support of resiliency factors and the development of preventive measures such as changing gender socialization patterns and structures of power relationships in the family and in the society as a whole.

Finally, it is important to remember that intervention with child witnesses plays an important role in the construction of their fate into a social problem (Loseke, 1987). Advocating for these children by raising the public's awareness about the damaging effects of witnessing violence will necessarily label them as a deviant population. As such, child witnesses of domestic violence will have to cope throughout their lives with both the aftermath of witnessing violence and the implications of the socially deviant label attached to them. Hence, it is suggested that practitioners be extremely attentive to possible misuse of dramatic, generalizing descriptions of child witnesses of domestic violence. In the next section, we review existing intervention programs developed to help child witnesses cope with the violence and its consequences.

❏ Intervention With Children of Battered Women

Women's concerns for their children and the growing awareness of the effects of violence on children have led to a variety of new services for children (see Peled, Jaffe, & Edelson, 1994). Early in the history of battered women's shelters, child counseling often was delivered on a one-to-one, informal basis. As shelters and other nonresidential domestic violence programs have grown, many have developed formal programs to address children's needs. A few treatment procedures with individual children were suggested (Arroyo & Eth, 1995; Black & Kaplan, 1988; Davies, 1991; Silvern & Kaersvang, 1989; Silvern, Karyl, & Landis, 1995). Most services, however, included the provision of small support and educational groups in which children "break the secret" of family violence. A survey of federally funded demonstration projects for children in battered women's shelters found that "the service most commonly recommended for the children was counseling, most often group counseling and play therapy" (Layzer et al., 1986, p. 4).

GROUP PROGRAMS FOR CHILDREN

There is a small but growing literature on groupwork with children of battered women (see Alessi & Hearn, 1984; Cassady et al., 1987; Gentry & Eaddy, 1980; Gibson & Gutierrez, 1991; Grusznski, Brink, & Edleson, 1988; Hughes, 1982; Johnson & Montgomery, 1990; Ragg & Webb, 1992; Wilson, Cameron, Jaffe, & Wolfe, 1986). Such groups are offered in shelters, safe-homes, family court clinics, and outpatient social service agencies (some of which focus exclusively on domestic violence).

The groups described met for 60- to 90-minute weekly sessions for 6 to 10 weeks. The number and frequency of sessions in shelter programs often depended on the child's needs and length of stay. The ages of child participants varied from 1 to 16 years, but most groups focused on 4- to 13-year-olds who were divided into groups according to age or developmental abilities. Reported groups also appeared to be small, and membership in most cases ranged from three to six children.

The great majority of these programs reported highly structured sessions with specific goals and educational activities designed to achieve these goals. The stated goals included helping child participants (a) define violence and responsibility for violence; (b) express feelings, including anger; (c) improve communication, problem-solving, and cognitive coping skills; (d) increase self-esteem; (e) develop social support networks; (f) develop safety plans; and (g) enjoy and feel safe in the group sessions.

These goals were achieved through a variety of structured educational and play activities that included presentations, discussions, modeling, role playing, art projects, homework assignments, and in one program (Gentry & Eaddy, 1980), a Family Night during which children's activities would take place either concurrent to a parent program or with parent participation.

Evaluation of Group Programs. Only a few evaluations of group programs have been reported in the professional literature. Jaffe, Wilson, and Wolfe (1986) reported a small pilot study that showed group intervention to have some success in changing children's self-esteem, attitudes about violence, and practical skills in emergency situations. Cassady et al. (1987) failed to find a clear pattern of results in an analysis of a small data set from a shelter-based group program.

DAP recently completed a 2-year qualitative evaluation of its children's program (see Peled & Edleson, 1992), and many of our findings have been incorporated into this manual. DAP's study was designed to fill the gap in knowledge about such interventions by providing a thorough analysis of one nonshelter group program from the multiple perspectives of those involved with it.

Qualitative evaluation was most appropriate for this project because of the following conditions: (a) Vague and general program goals required goal-free evaluation, (b) the agency context required an evaluation method that was least intrusive and that enhanced staff involvement, (c) in-depth information on the processes and quality of the program was needed to improve it, (d) side effects and unintended results were anticipated, (e) the use of standardized measurements with children may be obtrusive and limit the depth of data generated, and (f) the scarcity of empirical information on both the results and dynamics of these groups provided a limited basis for the construction of valid and reliable standardized instruments.

Data collection for this study included interviews with 30 children who participated in 8 groups, 16 mothers, 5 fathers, and 9 group leaders and administrative staff at the agency. In addition, one complete group process (10 group sessions and 3 family sessions) was observed. The in-depth, semistructured interviews were conducted by two female interviewers using thematic guides specifically developed for this study.

One of the challenges of this evaluation was the interviewing of young children on an emotionally loaded subject. Several design factors were considered to maximize both safety for the child and his or her willingness to share thoughts and feelings about the group. Voluntary participation was stressed to each child and parent throughout the interviews. The interviews were conducted as a relaxed conversation, and the child was offered a variety of toys with which to play while talking with the interviewer.

The evaluation found that all children interviewed and observed achieved, to some extent, the complex goal of breaking the secret. Interviews and observations suggested that, at the end of the group and later on, most children could define abuse, distinguish among forms of abuse, and state that "abuse is not okay" and "the abuse is not my fault." Furthermore, a gradual process of emotional disclosure and learning to talk about feelings was evident for all children, though the pace and extent of this process were idiosyncratic to each child. Finally, many of the children shared some of their personal experiences with the group but seemed to be selective and controlled the amount and type of information they shared. Listening to their friends' personal stories, children discovered they were not the only ones whose family experienced violence. This discovery was especially meaningful for children who never before spoke openly about the violence in their homes and who felt ashamed, guilty, and confused about it.

The ability to break the secret of violence appeared to be dependent, to an extent, on the child's feelings of trust and safety in the group. The evaluation found that most of the children interviewed felt safe and comfortable at some point of the group process, though the time required to feel safe and the degree of trust varied. Some evidence also suggests that some of the children acquired self-protection skills and assertive conflict resolution skills.

Group participants learned new information and adopted new attitudes, thus relieving some of the pain and stress they brought with them to the group. However, findings also suggested that group processes, especially those involved in breaking the secret, produced new tensions within the children and among family members. The processes of sharing information and expressing feelings about the violence and turmoil at home were emotionally difficult and stress producing. Talking about violence that occurred in their homes required children to remember what happened, to peel away layers of defenses they constructed with time. Thus children were not only relieving but also reliving some of the pain and stress they brought with them to the group.

Information gained through the evaluation of DAP's children's program about group goals, group processes, and intended and unintended results of the group is used throughout this manual. In the next chapter, we present the goals and subgoals of the group program as identified by group leaders in the evaluation study.

2

Goals of the Children's Group Program

Group leaders at DAP's children's program identified four major goals for groupwork with child witnesses of domestic violence (see Box 2.1).

Each of these larger goals is most likely achieved through group processes designed to attain specific, expected changes among child participants. In Figure 2.1, we identify the group processes and the outcomes they are expected to achieve.

Box 2.1: Major Group Goals

- To "break the secret" of abuse in their families
- To learn to protect themselves
- To experience the group as a positive and safe environment
- To strengthen their self-esteem

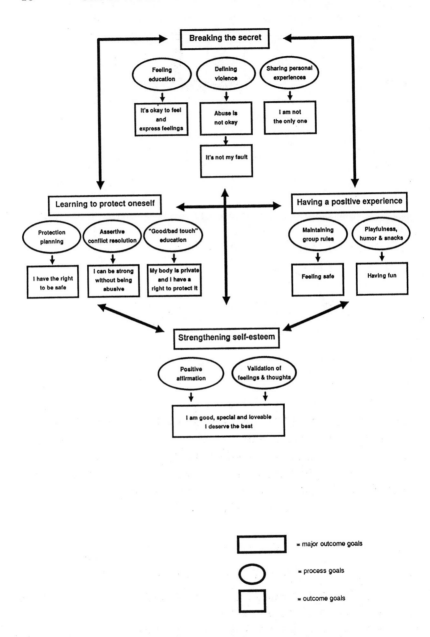

Figure 2.1. Process and Outcome Goals for Children's Group

Box 2.2: Subgoals of "Breaking the Secret"

- Defining violence → Abuse is not okay, and it's not my fault
- Feeling education → It's okay to feel and express feelings
- Sharing personal experiences → I am not the only one

A variety of group activities take place in any one session. Each of these activities reflects a "process"—for example, feeling education and assertive conflict resolution (see ovals in Figure 2.1). These activities, we hope, lead to specific emotional or attitudinal changes among the children attending the sessions (see boxes in Figure 2.1). These hoped-for outcomes, when taken together, should reflect achievement of the four major goals (see bold boxes in Figure 2.1). The processes and outcomes shown in Figure 2.1 are relevant and appropriate for all age groups, though the specific group activities used to achieve them may differ to some extent, depending on the developmental levels of group members.

Next, we describe the four major goals and address both the processes and outcomes derived from these larger goals.

❏ Breaking the Secret

"Breaking the secret" is a widely used metaphor for a common goal of intervention with victims of family violence (Saunders & Azar, 1989). The phrase alludes to the tangible nature of the emotional isolation that many children of battered women appear to experience (Roy, 1988) and to the work required in dealing with it. This goal is complex in terms of group processes and outcomes. It includes three group processes, each with a complementary outcome. They are listed in Box 2.2.

DEFINING VIOLENCE → ABUSE IS NOT OKAY,
AND IT'S NOT MY FAULT

Starting with the second group session, children learn to define violence and to distinguish among different kinds of abuse. Group leaders actively help child participants gradually acquire "violence vocabulary," which allows them to talk about abuse, share abusive experiences, and assign responsibility for abusive behavior. For example, children learn the word *abuse*, the differences between abusive and nonabusive behaviors, and what physical, emotional, and sexual abuse are. These processes also enable children to learn that abuse is not okay and that it is not their fault when someone is abusive to them or when other people abuse each other.

FEELING EDUCATION → IT'S OKAY TO FEEL
AND EXPRESS FEELINGS

Breaking the family secret often involves children opening up and expressing the full range of emotions triggered by their exposure to violence. Through "feeling education," group leaders work with children on awareness of different feelings, labeling feelings, and the range of ways people express feelings (e.g., through verbal expression, crying, holding feelings in, acting out, violence). The legitimacy of all feelings and of their appropriate expression is continually reaffirmed.

Feeling education starts in the first session, when children are asked to say how they feel about coming to the groups and continues throughout the group. Particular emphasis is given to the feeling of anger, which is the focus of the third session.

SHARING PERSONAL EXPERIENCES → I AM NOT THE ONLY ONE

After discussion of violence and related emotions, children are encouraged, toward the middle of the group (fourth to sixth sessions), to start sharing their own personal violent experiences in their homes. Listening to their friends' stories, group members discover they are not the only ones whose family has experienced violence. This discovery is especially meaningful for children who never before have spoken openly about the violence in their homes and who feel ashamed, guilty, and confused about it.

Box 2.3: Subgoals of "Learning to Protect Oneself"

- "Good touch-bad touch" education → My body is private, and I have the right to protect it
- Assertive conflict resolution → I can be strong without being abusive
- Protection planning → I have the right to be safe

❑ Learning to Protect Oneself

The emphasis of this relatively short group program is on emotional and attitudinal changes. The ability to achieve behavioral effects is rather limited. Still, the children's reality, a potentially life-threatening one, at a minimum requires self-protection training. Such training includes three processes, each with a complementary outcome (see Box 2.3).

"GOOD TOUCH-BAD TOUCH" EDUCATION → MY BODY IS PRIVATE, AND I HAVE THE RIGHT TO PROTECT IT

In the seventh session, group members are provided basic definitions and an understanding of physical and sexual abuse and are taught basic protective skills. In addition, the issue of sexual harassment may be addressed. The information provided on abuse is aimed at prevention and is not sufficient as the sole intervention with children who were sexually and/or physically abused.

ASSERTIVE CONFLICT RESOLUTION → I CAN BE STRONG WITHOUT BEING ABUSIVE

Assertiveness is the focus of the eighth session. It is important that children be aware of conflict resolution strategies as an alternative to the violent ones they have witnessed in their homes. Assertiveness also allows children to protect themselves and their rights in an appropriate manner, though only modest behavioral change should be expected in the light of group time constraints.

PROTECTION PLANNING → I HAVE THE RIGHT TO BE SAFE

In the ninth session, we conclude the children's work on self-protection by helping them develop a personal protection plan. Protection-planning activities take place toward the end of the group so that they can build on children's previous group experiences of defining abuse, talking about personal situations, and gaining a better understanding of the violence in their homes.

The aim of personal protection planning is to equip children with some practical and realistic skills to be used in emergencies. We hold parents and other adults in a child's life to be responsible for the child's safety and well-being. However, under the circumstances of family violence and dangerous situations in which a child's safety is at risk, we want the children to know that they also need to take care of themselves. Children need to be able to protect themselves from risks both inside and outside their homes.

❑   **Having a Positive Experience**

Often taken for granted, the universal goal of having a positive experience is very important for the success of groups for children of battered women. A positive experience is achieved through two processes and their corresponding outcomes (see Box 2.4).

The children's feelings of trust and safety in the group are a precondition for breaking the secret; fun activities provide children with an immediate gratification that balances the "heavier" violence-related aspects of the group. In this way, group processes involved

---

Box 2.4: Subgoals of "Having a Positive Experience"

- Maintaining group rules → Feeling safe
- Playfulness, humor, and snacks → Having fun

Box 2.5: Essential Rules for Group Participants

- Confidentiality (with the exception of suspicion of child abuse)
- No physical or verbal abuse or coercion
- Respect for other's opinions, feelings, and personal space

---

in providing a positive experience may contribute to the achievement of other major goals.

MAINTAINING GROUP RULES → FEELING SAFE

Group rules are established in the first session and maintained throughout the group. We consider three "essential rules" (see Box 2.5).

Rules allow clarity and predictability, which are basic components of a safe environment. Such an environment is especially important for child witnesses who have experienced emotional and physical threats and abuse. However, rules need not be overemphasized; as few rules as possible, and only realistic ones, should be established.

PLAYFULNESS, HUMOR, AND SNACKS → HAVING FUN

Initially, many children perceive the group as a serious, threatening place; some of them do not come of their own free will, but rather are "strongly prompted" to do so by their mothers. Group leaders are challenged to transform these initial feelings of apprehension and resistance into an enjoyable and attractive experience. Although one part of this transformation depends on the development of trust and familiarity with the people in the group, it is crucial that the children also have fun in each of the group sessions. At the same time as being educational and therapeutic, the group is also a social setting in which children make new friends, play, and eat snacks. Positive experiences in the group provide immediate gratification to children and also may contribute to enhancing their self-esteem.

Box 2.6: Subgoals of "Strengthening Self-Esteem"

• Positive affirmation
• Validation of feelings and thoughts
→ I am good, special, and lovable, and I deserve the best

❏   **Strengthening Self-Esteem**

Like most children in our society, children of battered women often are disempowered. They also may feel different from other children and sometimes are themselves abused. It is hoped that participation in the group will empower the children and strengthen their self-esteem. Strengthening children's self-esteem is influenced directly by two processes that lead to one general outcome (see Box 2.6).

Children of battered women may feel different from other children.

General supportive and validating interaction with group leaders occurs throughout the group. For example, many group sessions end with an affirmation of a positive quality of each child. Children's self-esteem may also be strengthened through the achievement of other major goals. As shown in Figure 2.1, major goals and results are interdependent and are depicted better as an interactive system, rather than as separate units. In this way, the goal of strengthening a child's self-esteem also may be an outcome of the other three major goals and contribute to their achievement. First, the process of breaking the secret tends to reduce children's shame, guilt, and isolation associated with the violence. Second, through learning to protect themselves, children are empowered and their confidence in their own skills is strengthened. Third, a positive experience in the group usually translates into a positive experience of themselves, of their capacities to be respected and cared for, and to be part of a positive, enjoyable interaction.

❏ **Achievement of Group Goals**

For some children, positive changes appear to come relatively easily and are more noticeable to parents and others in the child's environment. For other children, the group is a first and crucial step in a longer journey of healing, and behavioral changes appear more slowly and are harder to identify. Individual differences in achieving goals are likely to arise from a multiplicity of factors, such as the children's personalities and histories, group leaders' personalities and training, and group composition.

> *The group may produce new tensions within children and among family members.*

The group also may produce new tensions within children and among family members. These mostly unintended results are an essential component of the change process.

❏ **Healing and Stressful Influences of the Group**

In our evaluation study, we found that the groups produced not only healing effects, but also stress for the participating children. Furthermore, both of these results—healing and stress—were not confined to the children, but rather reverberated in significant ways through their families.

A graphic conceptualization of the intricate dynamics of healing and stressful influences of the groups is presented in Figure 2.2. Groups produced stress and healing effects through three sources (see Box 2.7; see also circle rim in Figure 2.2).

Box 2.7: Sources of Group Stress and Healing Effects

- The group as an event in the lives of the child and family members
- Group processes and activities
- Group intended results

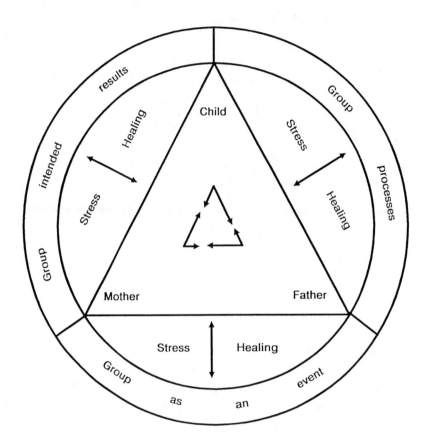

Figure 2.2. Healing and Stressful Influences of Children's Group

Each of the three sources has a dual influence not only on the participating child but also on his or her family—mainly on the parents, but sometimes also on siblings and members of the extended family (see triangle corners in Figure 2.2). Moreover, the group also influences the interactions between family members. Finally, in their turn, family members and the interactions between family members influence the group activities, processes, and outcomes, as depicted by the two-way arrows in Figure 2.2. As you can see, this is a complex feedback system of influence and interactions. In the following sections, each of the three sources of influence is briefly explained.

THE GROUP AS AN EVENT

The mere existence of the group in the lives of children and their family members and their participation in group and family sessions require them to confront and rethink violence-related issues. For example, some children perceive their group participation as an acknowledgment that something is wrong with them or with their families. On the one hand, these children often initially refuse to come to the group and may fight with their mothers over their group participation. On the other hand, mothers, on registration to group, may be immediately relieved of the worries and fears they felt regarding the impact of the violence on their children.

GROUP PROCESSES AND ACTIVITIES

The many group processes and activities (described in detail in Chapter 4) also can have a dual influence of healing and stress on the child and his or her family. For example, the norm of confidentiality is one of several group rules aimed at facilitating feelings of safety and trust. As described by a 9-year-old boy, "One of the rules that I think was best was whatever is said in the group, stays in the group." Although this norm contributes to the children's feelings of

Confidentiality can create a boundary between child and parent.

safety, it also can make parents feel curious, uneasy, rejected, and a loss of control when their children choose not to share with them their group experience. In this way, confidentiality can create a boundary between child and parent.

GROUP INTENDED RESULTS

Group intended results are those results of the group that correspond to the initial major goals. The intended results are positive and can be seen as healing effects of the group on the child and, indirectly, on family members. The achievement of intended results, however, also can be a source of stress. For example, children can use their violence vocabulary acquired in the group to criticize their parents'

Box 2.8: Opportunities for Parent Involvement

- An intake session
- A group orientation
- Parenting group
- A closing family session

---

behavior. One mother told us her 9-year-old daughter started to threaten her after the group, saying, "If you touch me, I'll turn you in for child abuse." Such comments can put parents in a stressful position and create tension in the child-parent relationship.

❏ Family Involvement in Group

As suggested above, children's parents are influenced by the group and have influence on its activities, processes, and outcomes. Hence, it is important to facilitate a constructive and helpful interaction between parents and group. Such interaction would maximize parents' positive contribution to their children's group experience and minimize group-related stress. Parents are involved in the groups in four major ways (see Box 2.8).

INTAKE SESSION

The general goals of the pregroup intake process (described in detail in Chapter 3) are to identify the needs of the child and the family, to determine whether the child can participate in a group, and to connect the family with resources inside or outside the agency that might meet their needs.

The intake is tailored to the developmental stage of the child and is divided into three parts. The first part consists of an interview with the parent (usually the child's mother) in the presence of the child. With this approach, the parent serves as a model for the child, thus

---

Box 2.9: Parenting Group Goals

- To provide information
- To challenge attitudes, values, beliefs, and assumptions
- To create new insights
- To develop parents' child-rearing skills

---

giving the child permission to talk about violence, in addition to helping the child prepare for his or her interview. The second part consists of an interview with the child without the presence of a parent. The third part is a discussion with the parent about the intake worker's recommendations for the child and the family.

GROUP ORIENTATION

The orientation session follows intakes but occurs before the first group session (see Chapter 4 for detailed description). It serves to introduce both children and parents to the agency, the group leaders, and the group program. Group structure, contents, and norms are reviewed to provide parents (usually only mothers) with initial information they may need in order to feel comfortable with their children's group participation. In this way, the orientation can prevent potential misunderstandings and frustrations caused by lack of sufficient information. Further and more detailed communication with parents regarding group activities and their potential effects on each child should be carried out during the 10 group sessions.

PARENTING GROUP

A 10-week psychoeducational parenting group is offered as a voluntary option for parents of those in a children's group (see Chapter 5 for detailed description). The purposes of the parenting group are listed in Box 2.9.

The first half of each session consists of an educational activity around the day's topic. In the second half, parents are given the opportunity to support each other by sharing child-related needs and concerns. In addition, the parenting group provides a convenient and safe setting for keeping parents informed of the weekly content of the children's groups and for discussing questions and concerns they may have regarding their childrens group experience.

CLOSING FAMILY SESSION

A family session takes place soon after the last session of the childrens group and is attended by the child and his or her parents (see Chapter 4 for detailed description). The purpose of this session is to review the group with the child, to discuss the influence of the group on the child, and to provide parents with recommendations for future services (if needed). It also aims to further facilitate open communication about violence-related issues between parent and child and to provide both parent and child with the opportunity to give their feedback to the group leaders.

A careful design and implementation of each of the four forms of parents' participation decreases the stress that a child's participation may create for parents by maintaining ongoing communication channels with parents and keeping them well-informed of their child's group.

We also recommend that the (past) abusive parent's involvement in the group be encouraged as much as possible. While *always* considering the safety of the mother and the child a first priority, the participation of the other parent in the intake, orientation, parenting group, and closing processes is important if the child sees this parent on a regular basis. When the other parent cannot be involved in the group because of safety or other considerations, group leaders should help the mother and child by discussing related concerns with them. The possibility of involving the other parent in the child's group experience is assessed in the intake process, which is the focus of the next chapter.

3

Intake and Assessment

Intake and assessment are critical components of this group program. In this chapter, we discuss intake procedures and other assessment issues for both children and their parents. The intake has three major goals (see Box 3.1).

Box 3.1: Intake Goals

- To determine whether the child can participate in the group
- To identify the needs of the child and the family and to connect them with resources inside or outside the agency that could meet these needs
- To empower children and their parents through sharing information about what is common in families in which domestic violence occurs, giving positive feedback, respecting children's and parents' feelings and perceptions, and helping children and parents realize they have choices

---

> **Box 3.2: Counselor Requirements for Assessing Children**
>
> - Competence and sensitivity in interviewing adults and children
> - A mix of patience, flexibility, creativity, and humor; and the self-assurance to admit ignorance and one's own limitations
> - A well-grounded knowledge of normal child development and psychopathology
> - A broad understanding of childhood environments: the nursery, middle school, high school, playground, religious and ethnic institutions, and geographic region
> - Familiarity with the possible sources of fantasy in the world of youngsters: current literature, television programs and movies, entertainment and sports figures of particular popularity, and current events that have particular poignancy for children. Children often draw on images, language, and characters from these worlds when discussing or expressing their feelings and attitudes. The counselor's ability to relate to and discuss these images will facilitate the creation of rapport with the child and a better assessment of needs.

We are aware that conditions in shelters may require a briefer, more condensed intake process and also may preclude the use of the group composition standards suggested in this chapter. We believe, however, that the goals and processes of the intake interview and the ideas on which group composition is based will be useful in any setting where groups for children of battered women take place.

❏ Counselor Requirements for Assessing Children

An adequate assessment of children generally will require the features listed in Box 3.2 (Diamond, 1988).

Beyond these general considerations, it is our hope that the intake counselor is in agreement with the theoretical and philosophical assumptions held by the Domestic Abuse Project (see Introduction). Particularly important are the assumptions listed in Box 3.3.

Box 3.3: Suggested Assumptions for Counselors

- Abuse is a result of unequal power in intimate relationships.
- Battering is a learned behavior and as such can be unlearned and replaced with more productive ways of interacting.
- Victims/survivors stay in the relationship for a variety of reasons, including fear, lack of alternatives, family and societal pressure, and economic and emotional dependency. They do not stay because they want or deserve to be abused. Domestic abuse is never the victim's/survivor's or the child's fault.
- Violence itself is not caused by a poor intimate relationship, job frustration, sexual problems, child-rearing problems, or substance abuse/dependency, although these factors are more likely present and will cause stress.
- Abuse hurts all individuals in the family setting, and intervention should be available to all members of the family.

Assessing child witnesses of domestic violence also requires that the counselor be knowledgeable of the potential impact that witnessing domestic violence has on children (see Chapter 1). Awareness of the dynamics of battering, including issues specific to abusers and victims/survivors, is important. These issues include those listed in Box 3.4.

General information can be found in many articles and books on woman battering (e.g., Dutton, 1992; Edleson & Tolman, 1992; Goolkasian, 1986; Lobel, 1986; Sonkin, Martin, & Walker, 1985; Walker, 1979; Yllö & Bograd, 1988). Information on specific services can be

Box 3.4: Knowledge Required of Counselor

- Dynamics of violent relationships (e.g., misuse of power and control, the cycle of violence theory)
- Emotional, cognitive, and behavioral reactions to victimizations
- Intervention alternatives for both batterers and victims/survivors

found in phone books and directories of social services. Such information is required for understanding child witnesses' exposure to and experience with violence at home. It also will help the counselor assess the level of dangerousness to which the victim/survivor currently is exposed and provide him or her with information on how to protect him- or herself.

Counselors should be clear about the conceptual framework out of which they operate and assess children and adults (e.g., feminist, medical, psychoanalytic, behavioral, or family systems models), as well as the influence of their personal experiences, biases, and prejudices (e.g., racist, homophobic, or ageist attitudes and beliefs; personal experiences with family violence). Because conceptual frameworks, attitudes, and personal experiences encourage interviewers to emphasize some behaviors and dynamics over others (Holtzworth-Munroe & Arias, 1993), it is important to make use of consultations with colleagues or a supervisor.

Hearing horror stories related to domestic violence, including child abuse, can be extremely difficult for the counselor. The counselor may feel emotionally overwhelmed and even have an impulse to rescue the child and punish those responsible for the child's suffering (James, 1989). In any case, it is strongly recommended that the counselor seek supervision or consultation to deal with such feelings so that they do not thwart working effectively with children and their parents.

❑ The Referral

We recommend that only children whose custodial parents have had some form of domestic abuse intervention should participate in the children's groups. It is our experience that group participation may put children in an uncomfortable or even dangerous position if their parents do not share, understand, or agree with the attitudes encouraged by the group. For example, one of the subgoals of the group is to teach children to define violence, to distinguish among different kinds of violence, and to learn that "abuse is not okay."

Hence, certain behaviors that were seen previously by the child as "normal," such as screaming, may be redefined in the group as abusive. Several mothers reported in our evaluation that their children used this new knowledge to criticize their behavior, thus putting the mothers in an uncomfortable and even stressful position. Furthermore, some parents may find the "antiabusive" responses of their children to be threatening, even to the point of further violence. Parents, and especially mothers, who have participated in domestic violence treatment themselves are likely to be familiar with and support the vocabulary and the attitudes taught in the children's program.

The children's program can be introduced to participants of women's domestic abuse groups, foster parents, child protection workers, shelter workers, and other professionals working with children and their families. Parents probably will be the primary referral source of potential participants in a community agency children's group. When introducing the children's program to parents, especially to victims/survivors, it is important to use a nonjudgmental, nonblaming approach to discuss the possible effects of witnessing violence on children. In an agency providing services for both battered women and their children, parents' familiarity with a member of the children's team may facilitate referral of their children to the children's program.

Although battering men also can refer their children to the program, attention must be paid to the possibility that a perpetrator will use the referral to exercise control over the victim/survivor. For example, if a perpetrator suggests that the victim/survivor enroll the children in the program and she refuses because she thinks the timing is not right, the man may use her refusal against her in a custody dispute.

After referral, the child's parent or primary caregiver can be asked to complete the Children's Service Request Form (see Appendix A). The form includes basic information on the parent and the child and on how the former can be safely reached. The form then is given to the intake counselor who, on the basis of a telephone interview with the child's parent or primary caregiver (or a face-to-face interview with the mother in a shelter), judges whether an intake or an outside referral is more appropriate.

❑ **The Phone Interview**

The phone interview is usually the first contact a child's parent (or primary caregiver) has with the children's program staff. (In shelters, the initial interview commonly is conducted face-to-face within the first few days of shelter stay.) This contact is a critical part of the intake-assessment process because it sets the stage for developing a working alliance with the parent. Ultimately, this process also affects the development of a therapeutic relationship with the child. The parent's feelings about the phone interview may influence the child's feelings and, consequently, the child's willingness to participate in the intake and in the group.

One goal of the phone interview is to learn about the family's living situation and current abuse status, major problems, concerns and special needs regarding the child, and whether group participation may put the child at risk. These information categories are covered by the Phone Interview Form (see Appendix A). Another goal of the interview is to determine the appropriateness of setting a child intake.

INTRODUCTIONS

Before calling the parent, be sure to find out from the Children's Service Request Form whether it will be safe to leave a message if the parent is not available. The phone interview is guided by the Phone Interview Form. It often begins by telling the parent who you are, the purpose of the call, and the estimated time it will take to complete the phone interview (approximately 15 to 20 minutes). Do not continue with the interview unless the parent has agreed to do it at this time. If needed, schedule another, more comfortable time for the phone interview.

If the parent has agreed to be interviewed, inform him or her of confidentiality and limits to confidentiality—mainly child abuse and "duty to warn" reporting (see further details below)—as early as possible in the phone conversation.

Parents frequently request that more than one of their children be assessed for group participation. If so, information may be collected

> **Box 3.5: Requirements for Child Intake**
>
> - The child is between the ages of 4 and 12 (see exceptions below).
> - The child's custodial parent has completed or currently is involved in a structured domestic abuse program (see exceptions below).
> - The child is reported to have witnessed domestic violence in his or her family.
> - The child's participation does not put him or her or the mother at a greater risk for being abused. For example, both mother and child can suffer partner's retaliation in cases in which the woman is currently in an abusive relationship and her partner strongly opposes the child's group participation.

at one time for all potential child participants, making the phone interview longer.

MAKING A DECISION REGARDING INTAKE

It is sometimes difficult to determine the appropriateness of setting a child intake on the basis of a short phone interview. The criteria in Box 3.5 need to be met before proceeding with an intake for this program.

Each of the conditions in Box 3.6 may require a referral to another program. Information on these conditions is gathered through the Phone Interview Form. From it, a decision on whether it is appropriate to set an intake for the child and parent or to refer them to another program can be made.

INTAKE-RELATED INFORMATION

If you decide to conduct an intake with the family, the information in Box 3.7 should be given to the parent or primary caregiver over the telephone.

Box 3.6: Criteria Suggesting the Need for Referral

- The child is reported to be suicidal or self-injurious.
- The child is reported to exhibit extreme behaviors, such as total withdrawal and lack of communication, hearing voices or seeing things that other people do not hear or see.
- There is knowledge or suspicion of sexual, physical, or ritualistic abuse or other severe trauma that have not been treated.
- There is knowledge of chemical abuse by the child.
- The child has language limitations or disabilities that cannot be accommodated by the agency (e.g., interpreter needed for child with hearing impairment, does not speak a language spoken by staff, access is limited for child with physical impairment).

Box 3.7: Information Given to Parents Prior to Intake

- Agency's philosophy (see DAP philosophy in Introduction for an example)
- Brief description of group goals and structure (including number of sessions, day of the week, time of day, and length of each session)
- Fees
- An explanation of the assessment process (including intake format, length, goals, time, and place)
- Whether a clinical diagnosis (e.g., American Psychiatric Association, 1994, *DSM-IV*) will be given. If a clinical diagnosis is given, inform the parent of the specific diagnostic procedure and of the potential consequence of having a clinical diagnosis for insurance purposes (e.g., present insurance policy may pay for treatment of certain conditions, but preexisting conditions may prevent purchase of new insurance in the future).

INVOLVEMENT OF CHILD'S OTHER PARENT

Although some referred children live with ongoing violence, others do not. In some families, the perpetrator has gone through a treatment process, is no longer physically abusive, and is interested in maintaining involvement with his children, trying to heal the consequences of the abuse. In the course of the telephone interview, an initial decision must be made regarding the involvement of the referring parent's partner and/or child's other parent in the intake process. This decision does not apply to shelter residents; the safety of both women and children precludes the involvement of the perpetrator in the intake or the group processes.

Although the question on the Phone Interview Form regarding child's and mother's safety is a general one, it may be necessary to explore further the emotional and physical safety of the parent and the child before making a decision: Has the abuser taken responsibility for the abusive behavior? Is current physical and emotional abuse directed toward the child or the parent? Does threatening and/or intimidating behavior continue? How do the parent and the child feel about the involvement of the child's other parent?

If there is an indication of moderate to high risk of injurious or lethal behavior by the abusive person, it is the duty of the counselor to warn the potential victim(s) and to employ crisis intervention strategies to prevent further violence (Ganley, 1987). Such indication may be evident already during the phone interview.

McNeill (1987) suggests that the counselor needs to monitor and assess certain indicators (see Box 3.8) for a potential violent episode.

We recommend that the child's other parent be, at minimum, informed of the intake if that does not endanger the child or other family members and if both mother and child think it is a good idea. If appropriate, the other parent can take part in the intake process even if this requires a separate interview. This inclusion will prevent the intake (and, later, group participation) from becoming another secret the child needs to keep. The other parent's participation also will contribute to the information gained through the intake (e.g., regarding family dynamics, child's relationship with father, father's willingness and ability to support the child).

Box 3.8: Indicators for Dangerous Behavior by Abuser

- A history of repeated violent acts or an incarceration for violent behavior
- The extent to which the person appears to have a violent plan, as distinguished from a violent fantasy
- Whether the person has the present ability to carry out the plan
- The specificity with which the person describes the plan
- Whether the person has targeted a victim or a victim is reasonably foreseeable in the light of knowledge in the counselor's possession
- Whether triggering events are attached to the plan that will cause the person to activate it on the occurrence of some condition
- Whether a dramatic or sudden change in the person's circumstances has occurred, such as divorce, loss of job, infidelity of a spouse, romantic rejection, failure in an educational setting, humiliation caused by a known person, or death of a loved one
- Whether any steps have been taken to execute that plan, such as purchasing weapons or other dangerous materials, buying an airline ticket to visit the intended victim, saving money toward the objective, sending threats to the victim directly or through third parties, or performing minor acts as a prelude to the intended grand finale

Sharing information gained from the victim/survivor with the other parent may be done only with her full consent and on the basis of an assessment of the possible consequences for her.

INFORMING THE CHILD ABOUT THE INTAKE

If you decide to invite the parent and the child for an intake, inquire whether the parent has informed the child of plans to enroll him or her in a group that deals with domestic violence. If the parent has done so already, ask specifically how the child was informed. This information will add insight into how the parent talks with the child—whether the explanation is age appropriate according to the reported developmental status of the child and whether the parent

Box 3.9: Tips for Informing Child on Intake

- Keep in mind the child's developmental stage by using words the child understands.
- Keep a relationship or family focus versus "child as the problem" focus (e.g., "We are going to get help so that we can all feel good about ourselves," rather than "You need to go so that you can learn to act better").
- Keep a positive attitude (e.g., "This meeting is going to be interesting, and the counselor is a nice person," rather than "This meeting is a drag, but we have to do it if we want you in the group").
- Do not use the intake or group as a threat (e.g., "If you don't behave yourself, you will have to go to group").
- Avoid statements that explicitly or implicitly blame the child for the abuse or imply that the child is "bad."
- Avoid comparing the child with the abuser (e.g., "You're just like your father, that's why you have to go to that group").

is motivated out of anger and frustration with the child. If the parent has not informed the child, inquire how she plans to do so.

Parents may need guidance on how to talk with their children about the upcoming intake. Tips for parents are listed in Box 3.9.

❏ The Intake Interview

INTAKE FORMAT

A semistructured approach is used in interviewing parents and children. The intake is guided by a Parent Interview Form for the parent and Child Intake Forms for the child, covering various information categories (see Appendix A). Although it is useful to cover all categories of information, it is expected that you will adapt the language of the forms to your personal style and to what you perceive to be the most understandable language for the parent and the child. It is also expected that you will deviate from the Child Intake Form by adding questions and by probing further when appropriate. A good intake resembles a flowing conversation, rather than a rigid question-and-answer session.

INTAKE GOALS

The aim of the child intake is to determine whether he or she can participate in group, is in need of additional services from your agency or other agencies (before, during, or after group), and whether special needs of the child can be met by the agency (e.g., needs related to disabilities, transportation, medical care).

With the parents, the intake is designed to achieve two major goals. First, we seek to determine whether the child can participate in the group and, if yes, what issues need to be dealt with prior to participation in the group. These issues include (a) father's opposition to the child's participation in group and what associated risks exist if the child participates and (b) circumstances that may interfere with attendance or arriving to the group on time (e.g., transportation issues, school hours, after-school activities, planned vacation, medical conditions).

Second, we seek to determine the special needs of the parent or family that may necessitate additional services from inside or outside the agency. Such needs may include (a) safe shelter and/or domestic violence treatment; (b) parent education; (c) support groups (e.g., Parents Anonymous, Adult Children of Alcoholics, Alanon, Alateen, incest survivors' groups, grief groups, women's groups, men's groups); (d) specialized treatment for any of the family members (e.g., substance abuse, sexual abuse, depression, behavioral problems, medical problems); and (e) financial and/or housing assistance.

Information on all of the above issues is gathered through the questions appearing on the Parent Interview Form and Child Intake Forms.

INTAKE STRUCTURE

The intake is divided into three parts. The first part consists of an interview with the parent in the presence of the child. With this approach, the parent serves as a model for the child, thus giving the child permission to talk about the violence, in addition to helping the child prepare for his or her own interview. The second part consists of an interview with the child, without the presence of the parent. The third part is a discussion with the parent about your recommendations. The child may or may not be present, depending on the results of the intake. The length of the parent and child interviews is usually 30 to 40 minutes each. The final recommendations part may take from 5 to 15 minutes, depending on your findings and the needs of the parent. Each of these components is discussed in the following sections.

PREPARING FOR THE INTAKE

When preparing for an intake, things to consider include the space to accommodate the number of adults and children who will be present, chairs for both adults and children (suitable for the child's size), sitting arrangements (allowing the child to sit close to the parent or play in a separate area of the room), and toys. If more than one child is being interviewed, it is best to arrange for two interviewers to enable careful observations of each of the children (see "Parent Interview: General Considerations and Strategies").

Several considerations are in order when preparing toys for the child to play with during the intake and in the waiting room. Select toys that are age appropriate, racially diverse, and that foster communication and creative expression (e.g., paper, drawing and writing utensils, puppets, a dollhouse, toy telephones, modeling clay). Children may be overwhelmed or distracted by a large selection of toys; hence, select toys with care. Bierman (1990) suggests that when interviewing an older child (especially a preadolescent), it may be desirable to have a few toys available (e.g., modeling clay or crayons) but to arrange them less conspicuously so that the child does not feel demeaned by being interviewed in a "nursery."

Intake Forms

Several forms are used during the intake. Samples of these forms are found in Appendix A. Before each interview, make enough copies of all the forms you will need. Having additional copies of the Release of Information Form is advised. A brief description of each of the Child Intake Forms is presented below, and further information on their use appears in the relevant sections below.

Permission to Treat Minors Form. This form informs parents of the legal status and duties of the counselor as a mandated reporter of child abuse and neglect. Parents are asked to read and sign the form at the beginning of the face-to-face intake interview.

Release of Information Form. This form authorizes the interviewer to obtain records (oral or written) from collateral services. It is completed by the interviewer and signed by the parent for each individual contact with a professional or a service.

When asking parents to sign a Release of Information Form, it is crucial that they understand what information will be shared, whether it is a one-way or two-way release of information, the purpose it serves, and how it will assist in better understanding and helping their child. Parents need to be assured that any information they wish to keep confidential (within the limits of mandated reporting) would not be shared with others.

Developmental Information Form. This form is completed by the parent for each of the interviewed children before the parent intake interview. It is reviewed by the interviewer, who then can decide whether further developmental information is required during the interviews with parent or child.

Parent Interview Form. This form guides the parent interview and is completed by the interviewer for each child considered for group. It covers areas related to family relationships, child behavior and relationships, parenting, violence directed at the child, and violence witnessed by the child.

Child Intake Forms. Three developmental levels are covered (ages 4 to 6, 7 to 9, 10 to 12). The forms guide the child interview and are completed by the interviewer. They cover areas related to school, interpersonal relationships (friends and family), self-concept, feeling states, child abuse, and violence witnessed by the child.

INTRODUCTIONS AND PRELIMINARIES

Before beginning the interview, we usually ask the parents to spend a few minutes completing the Developmental Information Form (see Appendix A) and quickly review it to get a sense of the child's developmental status and health. The form provides the interviewer with initial information regarding the child's developmental level and any communication issues that should be taken into consideration. For example, agitated behavior at the time of the interview by a child who is reported to suffer from attention deficit disorder may be assessed differently from a similar behavior by a child who is not known to suffer from any health problem.

Once everyone is settled in, explain the intake process to both parent and child even if the parent already has explained to the child what will take place. Having both parent and child present during this explanation provides an opportunity for the parent to view the interviewer's approach and manner of speaking to the child. As we stated earlier, if two children are to be interviewed, it is best to have two interviewers; each interviewer notes observations and interviews one child.

A child's unique pace and style of communication need to be considered by the interviewer. James (1989) suggests:

> Little children do not process ideas as quickly as adults and the manner in which they do process is more concrete than that of an adult. Since a child (especially a young child) communicates primarily through action and touch rather than words, it is important to pause after points are made or questions asked. (p. 60)

The following is an example of such communication with the child as the counselor introduces himself at the opening of the interview:

> I help kids when there are problems in the family. . . . All the kids who come here come from families where there is fighting. My job is to help kids to talk about their feelings about the fighting.

Use language that is age appropriate and give permission to ask questions any time the child feels confused or does not understand.

Explain the interview structure after the above introduction. Include information about who will be interviewed first, where each interview will take place, and the approximate time of each interview. Note the child's reaction when told that he or she will be interviewed alone, that no parent will be present. The child can be offered toys or drawing materials to play or work with during the time the parent is being interviewed. Although the child may appear to be actively engaged in play, he or she often is paying attention to what is being said about him or her and other family members. Offer permission to listen so that the child does not feel as though he or she is eavesdropping.

Address the issue of confidentiality prior to the parent's interview. The parent needs to read and sign a Permission to Treat Minors Form (see Appendix A), which discusses legal confidentiality and mandatory reporting laws. In addition, it is important to clarify the agency's standards of confidentiality as they relate to (a) access of other professionals inside and outside the agency to the intake material, (b) access of the other parent or primary caretaker to the intake material, (c) sharing parent intake information with the child, and (d) sharing child intake information with the parent. Confidentiality can be discussed with the child when interviewing him or her (see "Child Interview: General Considerations and Strategies").

Some parents would prefer not to share certain information about their abuse or other conditions in their child's presence. It is important to let parents know before the interview starts that this preference is legitimate and that they will be able to discuss such information with you at another time (e.g., over the phone, in a separate session).

PARENT INTERVIEW: GENERAL
CONSIDERATIONS AND STRATEGIES

The parent interview is based on the Parent Interview Form (see Appendix A). Have additional paper available to write down direct quotes or comments made. These notes can be organized later in the intake summary. As a general rule, document what the parent reports, rather than what you interpret her to be saying.

If both parents are present, the same Parent Interview Form can be used; however, it is important to note on the form the source of information (mother or mother's partner/child's father). Encourage parents to express respectfully any difference of opinion with each other.

It is important to observe parents individually and as a team. Parents' interaction and communication with you and with each other can be informative. Pay attention to behavior that is likely to affect the child. For example, parents may never refer to each other when answering questions, but rather seek the child's confirmation for some of their answers. Notice how parents share in telling their concerns, who dominates, and whether one parent is trying to get you on his or her side. Note parents' attitudes toward historical information related to the violence, as well as convergent and divergent views between them.

> *Be especially sensitive to controlling and abusive behavior.*

Be especially sensitive to controlling and abusive behavior. This information will help you assess the safety needs of the mother and the child. If the man's behavior is controlling to the point of intimidating the woman and blocking her ability to express herself, stop the interview and comment on this situation. For example:

> I would like to stop the interview here. I am aware that you do not allow your partner to express her thoughts and feelings without interfering. This feels like an unsafe situation to me, and I would prefer to continue the intake separately.

Also note any signs in the parents' appearance, behavior, or communication that may indicate problem areas (e.g., acute stress or anxiety, extreme poverty). At the end of the interview, you may want to share your observations with the parents and ask them whether they are interested in discussing it or in receiving help.

Be mindful that the child is in the room. Pay attention to his or her reactions to parental disclosures. Note when the child interrupts, talks under his or her breath, acts out, and the like. For example, when questions are anxiety provoking for the child or when the child senses a parent's discomfort, distracting behavior may be initiated. This also holds true if two or more children are in the room. This information can be used for assessing the child's ability to discuss the violence. You may also be able to gain insight into specific roles the children play in their family (e.g., scapegoat, victim, pleaser, peacemaker). The child may take on similar roles in the group.

Also be aware of parents' sensitivity to the presence of their child in the room. Note their communication with the child and about the child: Are they encouraging, supportive, and empowering, or are they negative, shaming, angry, and critical? Are they respectful of the child's physical and psychological boundaries, or are they intrusive? Do they set appropriate limits in the interview when the child distracts or acts up? Are they disciplining or punishing? Is their discipline age appropriate and logical? This information will help you further assess the possible need for parent education and whether the child is abused or neglected.

We believe that physical discipline is counterproductive and creates an association between anger and violence. When we discuss with parents their discipline methods (Questions 19 to 21 on the Parent Interview Form), we tell them that we believe hitting is never okay and that this is the message we give children in the group. It is our experience that some children who participate in our groups start challenging their parents' choice of discipline methods when these are abusive or violent. We let parents know about this possibility and discuss with them their anticipated reaction to such a challenge from their child.

If parents use physical discipline (e.g., spanking), we ask them to commit to replacing it with nonphysical methods. We help them with suggestions for alternative discipline methods and may recommend books, support groups, or other appropriate resources.

Parents may feel anxious during the interview. This anxiety may be related to feelings of guilt about their child's difficulties. We let abusive parents (and partners) know that we hold them responsible both for the abuse they have committed and for stopping it. At the same time, however, we acknowledge parents' anxiety and give them a supportive message. It is important that parents do not feel judged harshly by you. If you sense parents' guilt, you can initiate discussion on this topic by normalizing this feeling (e.g., "A lot of parents I see often feel guilty. I wonder if this has been your experience?").

Parents' description of their child's behavior may be influenced by their own guilt, shame, anxiety, or anger at the child for his or her misbehavior. Consider obtaining information from other sources familiar with the child (e.g., teachers, school counselor/psychologist, medical doctor, day care provider). Ask direct questions and encourage parents to expand on areas that seem confusing or contradictory, that evoke disproportionate feelings, or that were avoided earlier.

At the end of the intake, encourage parents to call you with important information they forgot to report during the intake or chose not to share at the time because of their comfort level with you or because of the child's presence.

CHILD INTERVIEW: GENERAL CONSIDERATIONS AND STRATEGIES

Preliminaries. The first task in interviewing the child is to get the child to go with you into the interview room (e.g., a playroom or prearranged office) of his or her own free will. If the child is unwilling to separate from the parents, do not force him or her to go with you; this could be especially frightening for children who have witnessed violence and who have lived in an unpredictable and highly controlled world. Some of the child's fear may dissipate when his or her feelings or experience is mirrored back (e.g., "I can see that you are scared," "I can see that you don't want to go with me"). Avoid a power struggle with the child; rather, invite the child to check out the playroom with you. Giving the child permission to leave the interview room at any time to check on the whereabouts of his or her parents also helps decrease the child's anxiety. Discuss this arrangement with parents so that they can be available to the child during this time. If the child is unwilling to separate from a parent, you may want to conduct the interview in the parent's presence.

Once in the interview room, observe how the child explores the room. Is he or she inhibited, spontaneous, impulsive, aggressive, anxious, or needing permission to explore? This may be a clue to how the child enters his or her world in general or a new experience in particular. Pay attention to the child's apparent level of anxiety. If the child is very anxious (e.g., talks fast or abruptly changes the subject, moves away from you, throws things, wrings hands, hides under furniture), you may want to start by helping the child feel more comfortable. This can be done by empathizing with the child's situation, offering a drink, and suggesting that he or she draw or play for a while. When doing this, consider the child's developmental level, emotional capacities, and other information obtained in the parent interview and from the Developmental Information Form.

Confidentiality. It is best to tell children from the outset about limits to confidentiality. This can be done in a matter-of-fact way in simple language:

> Everything we talk about in here is private. I won't repeat things that you tell me to anyone unless I get worried about a few things. I will have to tell someone if I think you are hurting yourself, hurting someone else, or if someone is hurting you, including your parents or brothers and sisters. Hurting means different things like hitting or touching on private parts of the body. (Gil, 1991, p. 49)

The child should be given permission to ask questions for clarification. Avoid making promises or predictions about a particular outcome: telling the child that he or she will get to stay in the home, that the abuser will not go to jail, or that the police will not interview him or her or come to school.

Dealing With Anxiety. Use the Child Intake Forms (see Appendix A) as a guide for the interview but be sensitive to the child's needs. Some children may feel threatened by your writing. You may want to explain to the child the purpose of writing down answers, negotiate a less threatening way of documenting the interview, or if all else fails, document the interview immediately after the intake. It is important that you be highly familiar with the intake guide questions so that, if required, you can pose them to the child from memory.

Interviewing children takes empathy, patience, and flexibility. Some children take longer than others to develop enough trust to let you into their inner world. It is important to respect the pace of the child and not attempt to force the child to talk by continuing with intrusive questions. You may want to select a game or another concrete activity to help the child feel more at ease while answering your questions.

If a child becomes particularly anxious or nonresponsive at some point during the interview, you may introduce puppets, dolls, toys, or stuffed animals to help him or her talk about difficult subjects. Such interventions provide a measure of safety and emotional distance from the interviewer or subject matter. You may begin, for example, by talking with a puppet and asking other puppets to come over and talk with you on the child's hands. Young children are usually quick to respond to this invitation. A conversation between two or more puppets then can follow. The child's puppet can talk for the child and about the child's experiences.

Children may feel safer and empowered when given instructions to indicate they are especially scared or need a break. That can be done by having the puppet show an agreed-on sign (e.g., a head motion, having the puppet bite its tail). Toy telephones—one for the child and one for the interviewer—also can be used to allow the child to talk about things that may be too threatening to say face-to-face. A dollhouse is another useful tool for helping children describe their worlds (MacFarlane & Waterman, 1986).

Interviewing Strategies. It is important that the child interview be noncoercive. Noncoercive interviewing is crucial for the protection of vulnerable interviewees, such as children who have experienced traumatic events (Gilgun, 1989). In a noncoercive interview, the child chooses freely to provide data and has the freedom to withdraw at any stage of the intake. Although the child may not have a choice about coming to the agency for the intake, he or she has the right to choose not to talk with us at all or about certain issues. Giving the child as much control as possible is expected to empower and provide him or her with security. It is your responsibility to provide a setting in which free choice is possible. This may be done by telling the child the following at the beginning of the interview:

> During our meeting, I am going to ask you all kinds of questions. Some of them may make you feel uncomfortable. But I would like you to take good care of yourself and be in charge of letting me know if things get to be too uncomfortable. You don't have to answer any question

if it doesn't feel good to do it. You can also ask me at any time to take
a break or to finish our meeting.

It is also important to remind the child about these rights (not to
answer a question, to take a break, to end the interview) whenever
he or she seems to be under stress during the interview.

The child interview should focus on the child's feelings and internal experiences, areas in which the child is the most reliable inform-
ant. Interviewing strategies should match the child's developmental
status (e.g., how you say things, vocabulary used, type of examples
used). As a general rule, use more concrete questions and examples
with younger children.

Document what the child says and what you see, rather than
interpreting what you think the child means. It is always best to
inquire openly how children feel or how they perceive their world,
rather than using suggestive questions. Using comments rather than
direct questions may result in greater disclosure—for example, "Hmm,
I wonder what that would be like," or "I wonder what other feelings
might be there."

When asking the child questions related to feelings (e.g., "How do
you feel when they fight?"), you may use simple drawings depicting
happy, sad, angry, and frightened expressions (Bierman, 1990). Ask the
child to label each face and then to point to one of the faces or to show
how he or she feels in this particular situation. When faces are used in
this fashion, no oral response is required from the child, thus making
the task easy and fairly nonthreatening even for young children.

If the child appears comfortable and capable of more extended
inquiry, you may explore the child's answers further with simple
probes. For example, if the child points at a sad face as his or her
feeling "When mom and dad fight," you may wish to ask follow-up
questions, such as: "What about that makes you sad?" "Does it just
make you sad, or does it make you a bit mad or scared too?" "What
do you think might happen when you hear them fight?" Pay close
attention to the child's responsiveness when answering these questions; it will indicate whether you can probe further or need to take
a less threatening line of inquiry.

Although you may want to comfort children physically after disclosure of traumatic experiences, it is best to suppress this spontane-

ous gesture. This is especially true for children who have been physically abused and, thus, betrayed with unwanted touch. It is possible to hold children emotionally without physically touching them.

To the extent that areas of significant distress were explored, the child may feel, at the end of the interview, somewhat upset and disorganized. It is helpful, then, to provide the child with a period of nonthreatening free play or nonintrusive activity to allow him or her to regain composure. In addition, you may use this period to provide an atmosphere of positive regard and interpersonal support for the child (Bierman, 1990).

It is important that the child leave the interview feeling respected and valued—or in children's language, "feeling good"—as this most likely will increase the likelihood of the child's willingness to return.

Interviewing Abused Children. It is estimated that 30% to 40% of children who witness violence at home are also victims of sexual and physical abuse (Hotaling & Straus, 1989). This percentage is even higher among shelter residents (Layzer et al., 1986). A suspicion of abuse may arise during the intake interview, and as a mandated reporter, it is your responsibility to create an atmosphere of safety and acceptance in order to facilitate the screening process. Child abuse and neglect are "the physical or mental injury, sexual abuse or exploitation, negligent treatment, or maltreatment of a child . . . under circumstances which indicate that the child's health or welfare is harmed or threatened thereby" (Federal Child Abuse Prevention and Treatment Act, 1974).

General Considerations. Be aware of possible indicators for sexual and physical abuse and their manifestations at different ages. Remember that, with few exceptions, sexual abuse cannot be inferred from behavioral problems (for more information on possible indicators for sexual abuse, see Haugaard & Reppucci, 1988; Salter, 1988). Regarding physical abuse, it is often hard to decide what to do when the actual injury is not "serious," especially if the parents claim they used their right for a "reasonable" corporal punishment. By definition, a parent who intentionally engages in "seriously harmful behavior" is not being "reasonable." This includes any punishment or assault that results in a broken bone, eye damage, severe welts, bleeding, or any other injury that requires medical treatment (Besharov, 1990). Physical punishments or assaults that do not create a danger of serious physical injury are nevertheless reportable if they amount to emotional abuse. (For more information on identification and reporting of child abuse, we recommend Besharov's book [1990] *Recognizing Child Abuse: A Guide for the Concerned.*)

Children may provide you with only pieces of information regarding their abuse. Remember that verbal skills are among the least developed skills of many young children and that children's thoughts and memories are usually not well organized and frequently come out fragmented and confused.

Be mindful of the power differential between you and the child; power and control are central issues in these children's lives. Use noncoercive interviewing and help children feel (and be) in control over what they share. Remind them that they can choose not to discuss things that are too painful and that they have the right to stop the interview if it is getting too difficult for them.

Educate yourself about the common emotional repercussions for children and parents after disclosure of sexual abuse and about the many aspects of the legal system that come into play after such disclosure. Familiarize yourself with relevant resources in your community because a referral is often necessary.

Interviewing the Child. When asked whether they have been touched in a private place or hurt in other ways, some children will communicate to you that they feel uncomfortable talking about it. Such a response may reflect the child's embarrassment, mainly regarding sexuality, or indicate the possibility of abuse. It is best to address the two possibilities directly. For example:

> I wonder why you are hiding behind the pillow.
> Pause
> Is it because it's embarrassing to talk about this?
> Pause
> Maybe you feel like it is a secret that you cannot talk about?

If the child indicates that he or she has a secret, you can start by talking about different kinds of secrets: "fun" secrets, such as surprise birthday parties, or "scary" secrets, such as someone hurting another person. Explore what, if anything, the child thinks will happen or has been told will happen if he or she tells. It is important to find out who may have threatened the child because it may not be the same person who abused him or her (MacFarlane & Waterman, 1986).

Respond in a calm voice and manner to statements indicating the possibility of abuse. Children are sensitive to subtle changes in the interviewer's behavior and body language and may shut down or adapt their behavior to lessen your reaction. An underreaction is generally safest with a scared child. It is a good idea to be prepared with a standard, nonjudgmental phrase when caught off guard (e.g., "And then what happened?") so that you will gain some time to think of another, more appropriate response than your gut reaction.

If a child indicates that he or she has had private parts touched or has been physically hurt in other ways, ask: "Can you tell me a bit more about that?" You also may want to acknowledge how difficult it is to talk about what happened and to remind the child that he or she does not have to tell you things if he or she does not want to. Allow children to tell you their own stories at their own pace and in their own words. Stick to open-ended questions. Be careful not to make any statements about the alleged abuser in the child's presence because children often retain positive feelings about their abusers. Children can be told that adults or big people sometimes get confused and do things to children they should not do and that these adults need help to get better (MacFarlane & Waterman, 1986).

MacFarlane and Waterman caution not to suggest to the child that anything about the interview is pretend, including asking the child to describe or show what has happened to him or her. Although the "let's pretend" game is much less threatening to the child, it may serve to discredit the child if subjected to legal scrutiny, as well as provide the child with an opportunity to deny any statements made during the "pretend interaction."

Because children frequently blame themselves for the abuse, be careful in your choice of words and avoid even the appearance of blaming or placing responsibility on the child. For example, asking a child whether she took her clothes off, as opposed to whether she had to take off her clothes or someone made her take off her clothes, implies two different messages.

Again, children should receive the message that the abuse is not their fault, that it is always the abuser's fault, no matter what the circumstances are. If asked "why?" you can respond:

> Because grown-ups know it's wrong; because they can say no to themselves and to kids; and because grown-ups aren't allowed to touch/hurt kids in those kind of ways. (MacFarlane & Waterman, 1986, p. 97)

If a child discloses abuse, do not say that everything will be okay and not to worry. The child quickly will see through this and have no reason to trust you. Do not make promises you cannot keep (e.g., "Daddy will not go to jail"). The child should not be prevented from knowing the next steps. Let the child know that you are going to report the abuse to child protection services and inform the child about the circumstances that may develop after the report. If the child is at risk for further abuse, help the child develop a minimal safety plan (e.g., whom to call, where to go).

Do not make promises you cannot keep.

How much to tell a child about what will happen next depends on the age of the child and his or her ability to understand the situation. The child needs to be told as much of the truth as the interviewer thinks the child can handle. Children should be told that they are not responsible for the abuse and that they are also not responsible for what will happen after the disclosure (Jones & McQuiston, 1989).

❑ **The Assessment**

CHILD ASSESSMENT

After completing the parent and child interviews, you should have a general understanding of the child's current level of functioning and developmental status; the child's strengths, coping skills, defenses, and vulnerabilities; the child's problems and/or parental concerns, and abuse status; and a general sense of how the child has been affected by witnessing violence in the family. This information will enable you to make decisions regarding (a) the child's group participation and (b) the need for further assessment, for additional counseling prior to or in conjunction with group participation, and for other services related to special needs of the child.

General Considerations. Despite findings that predict consequences for children who witness violence, it is necessary to look at child witnesses of violence as individuals who have been affected by the violence in variable ways. As described in Chapter 1, many elements may play a part in how the child is affected: severity of violence witnessed, child abuse, gender of child, age of child, race of child, maternal stress, quality of child rearing, family dynamics, time of exposure to violence, and impact of shelter residence. Factors that may mediate the impact of the abuse are internal coping strategies and external support, biological development, and social development. Hence, you need to be mindful of each child's unique configuration of vulnerabilities and capabilities (for a detailed discussion of children's experiences of witnessing violence, see Peled, 1993).

Behavior is complex and is determined by multiple factors. When observing a child's behavior, avoid oversimplifying or attributing a single cause to a discrete behavior. "Jump" to hypotheses before jumping to conclusions. Take the Greenspans' advice: "Having an unusual feeling is a clue to a diagnostic question, rather than an indication of any conclusion" (Greenspan & Greenspan, 1991, p. 25).

Consider other bases (e.g., biological) as an explanation for the child's behavior. For example, conditions such as attention deficit disorder and hyperactivity can be manifested through agitated or aggressive behavior, which can be mistakenly diagnosed as stemming from emotional anxiety. Be familiar with neurologists in your community for providing a referral if you think a child's behavior may be related to a neurological condition, rather than or in addition to emotional state.

Some children may resort to regressive functioning in the interview; others may feel a sense of self-confidence when apart from their parents or when challenged with a new situation. Research shows that children's behavior varies even in familiar settings, such as school and home (Bierman, 1990), so do not assume that the child's behavior is representative of his or her typical behavior. If you notice inconsistencies in how the child describes him- or herself, how the child behaves in the session, and how the parents describe the child, you might consider consulting with other professionals familiar with the child (e.g., teachers, school counselors, day care providers).

Chronological age may be a poor marker of reasoning abilities in emotionally charged domains. Children who have experienced a great deal of stress, conflict, or unpredictability are particularly likely to show immature or illogical reasoning (Bierman, 1990).

ASSESSMENT FOR GROUP PARTICIPATION

The groups described in this manual may not be the appropriate type of intervention for some of the children you will interview. It is our experience that certain children will not benefit from the groups (e.g., by not having the concentration required to participate in group activities) or may be hurt by group participation (e.g., by being labeled a "trouble maker" in the group after extreme acting-out behavior). Furthermore, group processes may be sabotaged by the inclusion of children who do not function well in groups in general or in this kind of group in particular.

Shelter counselors may not be able to select children for group participation, but rather have to work with all of the children currently residing in the shelter. Such circumstance may require some adaptations of group format and content.

We recommend several child and parent assessment guidelines in the decision regarding the inclusion of children in the group:

A. Child-Related Guidelines

Children who fall into the categories listed in Boxes 3.10 and 3.11 are likely to benefit from the groups. Children who fall into the categories in Box 3.12 may be inappropriate for group and may need to be referred, instead of or in addition to group participation, for

Box 3.10: Criteria for Including a Child in Group

A. The child is developmentally between the ages of 4 and 12, and he or she:

1. can separate from parent for the time of the group.

   Indicators: Child's ability to separate from parent during the intake interview, parent's report on child's separation behavior in other settings (Question 36 on Parent Interview Form)

2. can interact socially with other children in same age group.

   Indicators: Questions 15 to 17 on Parent Interview Form, questions in "Interpersonal Relationships" section of the Child Intake Forms

3. has an age-appropriate attention span.

   Indicators: Child's concentration during parent and child interviews, Question 18 on Parent Interview Form

4. can distinguish between thoughts, feelings, and behavior, and between self and others.

   Indicators: Child's ability to do so during the intake, Question 13 on Parent Interview Form

(continued)

individual therapy, further psychological evaluation, or to another specialized program.

B. Parent-Related Guidelines

The conditions listed in Box 3.13 are required for child participation in group.

COMMUNICATING RECOMMENDATIONS TO PARENTS

Decide whether it is appropriate to have the child present when you communicate your recommendations to the parents. Be prepared to talk to the parents in the presence of the child if there is no alternative supervision for the child in another room. You may also

---

Box 3.10: Continued

B. The child acknowledges violence witnessing.

The major goal of the group, as described in Chapter 2, is breaking the secret of violence. Children can begin pursuing this goal in group only if they acknowledge that violence has occurred in their families.

> Indicators: Questions in the "Violence Witnessed by the Child" section of the Child Intake Forms; Questions 30 to 32 of the Parent Interview Form

C. The child is not too active or passive.

Children who consistently act out in group settings, at school, and at home and who respond poorly to limits set by adults are not good candidates for group participation. The same is true for children who are consistently withdrawn and uncommunicative in such settings.

Children with these behavior characteristics are likely to have problems interacting with both peers and group leaders and may require more attention than group leaders are able to provide.

> Indicators: Children's behavior at the time of the intake; Developmental Information Form, questions in "Child Behavior and Relationships" section of the Parent Interview Form

---

consider setting another time to talk with the parents about your recommendations.

Review with the parents their presenting concerns. Note your observations, including the child's strengths and areas of weakness and how the former can improve the latter. Do not forget to note the parents' strengths as well. Inquire about any special needs of a parent or other family member that have not been addressed and that affect the child's or the parents' ability to follow the recommendations.

Box 3.11: Children Possibly Not Ready for Group

1. Children who are diagnosed as mentally ill or whose behavior indicates the possibility of problems such as severe depression, severe anxiety, dissociation or splitting under stressful situations, or severe post-traumatic stress

    Indicators: Child's behavior and responses in the intake; Developmental Information Form (particularly Questions 6 to 9); Parent Interview Form (particularly Questions 13, 27, 28, 30, 32)

2. Children who are self-injurious or suicidal

    Indicators: Question 29 in Child Intake Form (for ages 10 to 12 only); Question 28 of the Parent Interview Form

3. Children who have experienced and have not received treatment for severe or long-standing emotional, physical, sexual, or ritualistic abuse directed at them

    Indicators: Questions on abuse directed at the child on Parent Interview Form and Child Intake Forms

4. Children who are suspected of abusing alcohol, drugs, or other substances

    Indicators: Child's behavior during the intake; Question 28 on the Parent Interview Form

Box 3.12: Conditions Required for Child Participation

- The custodial parent has given permission for child participation in group (as indicated by signature on the Permission to Treat Minors Form).
- The custodial parent has completed or currently is involved in a structured domestic abuse program (see Phone Interview Form).
- The parent has given a verbal commitment to bring the child to group each week and to participate in the family session at the child's completion of group.

Box 3.13: Conditions Required for Couple/Family Therapy

- The abusive partner has completed a structured domestic abuse program, taken responsibility for his or her violent and emotionally abusive behavior, and does not currently exhibit any physically or emotionally abusive behavior toward his or her partner or other family members.
- The victim/survivor has completed his or her own structured domestic abuse program (but individual cases can be considered differently).
- The victim/survivor and the children feel emotionally and physically safe to be in the presence of the abuser.

You will need to decide whether you can draw a conclusion about the child's group participation from the intake information and before consulting with other professionals. If you think additional information, such as psychological testing or a medical examination, is necessary prior to making a decision, tell this to the parents. Explain to them how this information will help you make your decision and inform them who will review the results of the testing/ examination (it is usually the person who does them).

If you find the child appropriate for the group, inform parents about the start date and day and time of the group and make sure the child can attend the group sessions regularly and on time. If the parents know the child will miss more than two group sessions, it is advised to postpone the child's participation to another time. Also remind the parents about group goals, structure, and content.

From your observations, the intake content, or parents' direct requests, you may find that some parents may need or want counseling or other additional support (e.g., financial, legal, safe housing). Be familiar with professionals and agencies in your area that are sensitive to issues of children, parenthood, and domestic violence to which you can refer interested parents.

Some parents, especially in community agencies, may ask you to refer them for couple or family therapy. We recommend couple or family therapy only under the conditions listed in Box 3.14.

Disclosure of Abuse. It is your legal and ethical obligation to report knowledge or suspicion of child abuse to child protection services in your area. The injury must be sufficiently serious so that there is a danger to the child's "health or welfare." This limitation is meant to protect the rights of parents to exercise their best judgment about how to raise children and protect regional, religious, cultural, and ethnic differences in such beliefs (Besharov, 1990). Because child abuse laws vary from state to state, counselors are urged to familiarize themselves with the laws of the state where they practice (for more information on child protection response to children of battered women, see Echlin & Marshall, 1995).

If the parent being interviewed is reported by the child as the abuser, you will have to decide whether to discuss the abuse at this time, keeping in mind the child's safety considerations.

If the parent is not the suspected abuser, it is generally a good idea to give the child the option to tell his or her parent about the abuse while you remain in the room to support the child. If the child prefers you to be the spokesperson, he or she can choose to remain in the room or to stay in another room while you speak with the parent. You may decide also not to give the child a choice and to speak with the child's parent yourself, without the child in the room.

You can prepare the parent by saying that the child has something very important to tell him or her, that the child is acting especially bravely, and that it is crucial that the parent believe and support the child. Help the parent support the child by offering the suggestions in Box 3.15 (Jones & McQuiston, 1989).

Parents may respond to their child's disclosure of abuse differently. Common reactions are anger, outrage, helplessness, and guilt. For example, some may be angry at the child for various reasons: (a) They may feel betrayed because the child told a stranger and not them, (b) their feelings of fear and helplessness may come out as anger, and (c) some parents may feel guilty for not knowing or for not protecting their child.

Pay attention to parents' reactions and, when appropriate, explore their thoughts and feelings to get a better sense of what they might need. Inform the parents that you have to inform child protection services. You may want to encourage the parents to call too; this is a means for empowering the parents. You also may want to enable the

> **Box 3.14:** Tips for Parents Informed of Their Child's Abuse
>
> - Remain calm. Your child will interpret your outrage as your being upset with him or her.
> - Assure your child that he or she has done the right thing in telling.
> - Assure your child that the abuse is not his or her fault.
> - Tell your child that you believe him or her, that you will protect him or her, and that you are on his or her side.
> - Remember that the child may need continual assurance and validation.
> - Protect your child's privacy; siblings need to hear a brief, calm statement about what has happened.
> - Validate all of the child's feelings (e.g., guilt, anxiety, fear, confusion, shame, protective feelings for the abuser) even when they are different from your own (e.g., when the child expresses loving feelings toward the abuser).

parents to call child protection services in your presence or to be present when you call child protection services. Children may have mixed feelings about their parents calling: Some may be reassured; some may be upset. In the latter case, suggest that the parents call when the child is not in the room to hear the conversation (Jones & McQuiston, 1989).

Pay attention to parents' reactions and explore what they might need.

Before the family leaves, it is a good idea to give the parents permission to contact you if they have any further questions or immediate concerns. You may choose to give a referral at the time or wait until child protection services has investigated the case. Encourage parents to get support for themselves; consider giving parents a 24-hour crisis line number. Giving the child your business card serves as a token of the disclosure, to know that it really happened. A child also may want to call you with more information (Jones & McQuiston, 1989).

❏   **Group Composition**

A number of criteria are useful to consider when deciding which children will best compose a group. Some of these factors are specific to the model described in this manual; others are more general. These factors include group size, age, gender, race and ethnicity, siblings, sexual orientation of parent, disabilities, and physical and sexual abuse histories. Each of these factors is expanded below.

GROUP SIZE

We have found the optimal size for children's groups to be six to eight members (with two group leaders), depending on the maturity level of the participating children—the less mature the children, the fewer should be in the group. Less mature children generally need more individual attention and structure than more mature ones. Consider attrition rate when deciding the group size. It is our experience that an average of two children per group drop from the group before completion.

AGE

Generally, our groups are divided according to the age groups 4 to 6, 7 to 9, and 10 to 12. Because chronological age is not always a good indicator of the child's emotional and social maturity, the child's developmental status must be considered. Pay special attention to the child's social skills and ability to concentrate. Some children may need to be placed into a group in which they are chronologically younger or older than the majority of the group members.

GENDER

Having a balance in gender is optimal. When a child is the only male or female in the group, you will need to make a decision regarding his or her participation. Consider the child's personality, social and emotional development, relationships with children of the other gender (including siblings and friends), and the composition of the group as a whole. Consult with the child and the parents before making the final decision.

RACE AND ETHNICITY

We have found it best to have at least two children of the same race in a group. This inclusion stresses the multiethnic character of the group and may prevent a child in the minority from feeling alienated from the other members. If a child is the only member from his or her race or ethnic group, the child and parents should have a voice in deciding whether to include the child in the group. We usually will not wait for the parents to raise the issue, but rather initiate the discussion of it. Some children already may be part of a racial minority in their school or neighborhood and thus may be more (or less) willing to be a minority in group.

SIBLINGS

It is usually best to have siblings in separate groups; this separation generally provides the children with greater freedom to talk openly about their family and themselves. Having siblings in the same group may encourage the preservation of rigid family roles and dynamics and prevent the disclosure of secrets. Separating siblings may require having one sibling wait until another group forms or be included with a group of younger or older children. The latter should be done, however, only if it is also justified developmentally.

SEXUAL ORIENTATION OF PARENTS

Children of gay or lesbian parents may need to hide their parents' sexual orientation. This may especially be the case with lesbian mothers who are at risk of loosing custody over their children if their sexual orientation is disclosed to the children's fathers. Children also may feel embarrassed or confused about the sexual orientation of their gay parents. When these issues are compounded by the secret of domestic violence, it is more than likely that children of gay and lesbian parents will feel uncomfortable discussing family issues in a group dominated by children of heterosexual parents. For these reasons, we recommend you refer children of gay and lesbian parents to counseling or groupwork tailored specifically to their needs.

DISABILITIES

Because the initial phone interview serves as a screening process, it is assumed that children with disabilities who go through the intake process can be accommodated by the agency (e.g., interpreter for hearing and sight impaired, wheelchair accessibility). Children with disabilities are usually a minority population. Hence, you may not have had previous experience facilitating a group that included children with disabilities. Be honest with yourself and with your coleader about your comfort level in dealing with children who have disabilities. Children are perceptive and will sense your discomfort and may blame themselves for it. If you are not yet comfortable with the particular disability represented, we suggest you not facilitate the group until you have worked through your own issues on this topic.

PHYSICAL AND SEXUAL ABUSE HISTORIES

The group program in this manual has been designed for child witnesses of domestic violence. However, many child witnesses are physically and sexually abused themselves. Although some children who have been abused may be referred to other services after the intake, others who to some degree already have addressed their abuse in therapy may be appropriate for these groups. Children who disclose their own abuse during the group are not asked to leave and may be referred to another program at the end of the group.

As with other issues, we recommend that you not include only one abused child in the group. If a child is the only abused one in the group, he or she may feel different and alienated even around children who share the experience of domestic violence. It is important that an abused child hear during intake that some of the other children in the group may have been abused as well.

❏ **Conclusion**

This chapter provided a detailed description of the intake process. Identification and careful consideration of children's needs in the intake process is necessary for successful intervention with them. Skillfully conducted intakes also facilitate composition of groups that are likely to benefit the participating children. In the next chapter, we discuss the sessions composing the group program.

4

Group Sessions

This chapter provides a detailed description of the entire group program after intake. The group aims to achieve four main goals and their corresponding subgoals (see Chapter 2). The major goal of breaking the family secret is emphasized in the first six sessions. Ways of protecting oneself are discussed in the seventh and eighth sessions. Efforts to improve children's self-esteem and to provide them with a positive experience are central to each of the group sessions.

The Group Program

The group program includes an orientation, 10 core group sessions, and a postgroup family session. The presentation of each session includes a major theme or message, desired outcomes for the participants, an outline, and facilitator notes and food for thought. Each of these sections is described in Box 4.1.

Box 4.1: Sections of a Session Presentation

Group Message. This section describes the general theme of the specific group session. It reflects the larger goals of the program (as stated in Chapter 2) and guides the group activities. One can think about it as the desired answer a child (or a group leader) would give if asked, "What was the group about today?"

Desired Outcomes. This section defines concrete objectives for each session. We encourage group leaders to evaluate the achievement of these objectives for each child after each session (see sample Desired Outcomes Evaluation Form in Appendix B). By performing such evaluation, group leaders can keep track of a child's individual experiences in the group. It also may help increase the group leaders' awareness of concrete accomplishments by the child (see more details below).

Outline. This section is a summary of each session's activities. Many of these activities contain references to the numbered Facilitator Notes for that session.

General Considerations and *Facilitator Notes and Food for Thought.* These two sections provide further explanation and description of the outlined group activities and expand on the main issues dealt with in the session on the basis of data from the evaluation study we conducted (see Chapter 2). Items in "Facilitator Notes and Food for Thought" are numbered for ease of use.

The recommended group time for each session of the ten outlined is 1 hour for ages 4 to 6 and 1 hour to 1¼ hours for ages 7 to 12. Allow 1 hour for the orientation, and ½ hour for the family session at the end of the session.

We strongly recommend that each group be led by two counselors: a man and a woman. The presence of two group leaders in the room is required for optimal safety, support, and learning conditions. Male-female coleading provides opportunities for positive modeling of gender role behavior and male-female interaction and allows both boys and girls to relate to a same-gender and other-gender group leader.

As mentioned earlier, shelter conditions may not allow direct implementation of this group program, but rather require adaptation of some of the content and structure (for more information about shelter conditions, see Hughes & Marshall, 1995). Nonetheless, we believe that the experience- and research-based knowledge we offer here can be useful to counselors of children of battered women in a variety of settings.

In addition to the material reviewed in this chapter, an extensive bibliography of books and videos for children of battered women and for practitioners who work with them can be ordered through the Domestic Abuse Project of Minneapolis (see "Acknowledgments" for DAP's address).

OUTCOME EVALUATION

We recommend that you evaluate the achievement of the group's desired outcomes for each child after each session. The performance of such evaluation will help you keep track of children's individual accomplishments and experiences of the group. Such information is important for facilitating individual children's achievement of group goals and for an ongoing assessment of children's needs. It also can serve as an important source of information for assessing needs for further services at the end of the group.

Compare notes on children's outcomes with those of your co-leader and use the evaluation as a basis for team and supervisory discussion of children's individual progress and needs.

Child outcomes evaluation can be facilitated by evaluation forms based on the desired outcomes outlined for each group session. A sample of such a form (for the Orientation session) is provided in Appendix B. Similar forms can be created for each of the other group sessions. The following are suggested instructions for the use of such forms.

Instructions. Prepare a set of forms for each child in your group. Familiarize yourself with the desired outcomes prior to the session and pay attention to children's achievement of these outcomes during

**Box 4.2: Evidence Categories for Outcome Achievement
(partial list)**

General indicators:

- Participates/does not participate in group activities
- Talks/does not talk in group
- Brings things from home: food, toys, animals, etc.

Verbal indicators:

- Speech: tone, inflection, clarity, stuttering, pitch, etc.
- Verbalizes group message (knows what the group is about)
- Shares thoughts and feelings related to group activities
- Shares personal stories
- Asks questions on group material
- Aggressive: shouts
- Abusive: curses, threatens, puts others down, etc.

Behavioral indicators:

- Sits outside/inside the middle of the circle
- Hides in the room
- Leaves the room

(continued)

the session. Fill out the forms as soon after the session as possible, when your memory of the group processes is still fresh. Remember that you evaluate individual children, not the group as a whole. Evidence of outcome achievement can be both verbal and nonverbal. A list of common, not mutually exclusive, evidence categories is provided in Box 4.2.

Box 4.2: Continued

Behavioral indicators (continued):

- Devours/does not eat snack
- Aggressive: plays hard, slams doors, destroys toys, etc.
- Abusive: hits, kicks, punches, pulls hair, etc.
- Acts out/sits still

Social indicators:

- Social role in group
- Interaction with peers
- Interaction with counselors
- Interaction with parents and siblings

Body language indicators:

- Makes/does not make eye contact with counselors or the other children
- Agitated: paces, rocks, bites fingernails, has ticks, rings hands, cries, laughs, etc.
- Stiff/limp posture
- Facial expression: sad, depressed, lively, attentive, etc.

The achievement of some outcomes may be difficult to assess, especially when the outcome concerns a certain feeling state or cognitive change. A sensitivity to the child's individual manifestations of emotional states and cognitive understanding will be helpful. Write down additional observations of the child's experience in the session and other relevant information in the space provided under "General Comments."

Orientation for Parents and Children

❏ **Main Theme**

Introducing the agency, staff, and program.

❏ **Desired Outcomes for the Child and the Parent**

1. To become familiar with the agency, staff, and program
2. To wish to participate in the group

❏ **Outline**

Box 4.3: Orientation Outline

- Introduce the group leaders. (Session begins with parents, children, and all group leaders in the same room.)
- Introduce the program and the agency: Main goals of the group, group structure, time table, expectations from parents and children (confidentiality, child safety issues, being on time). [See Facilitator Notes 1, 2, 3, 4.]
- Have time for questions and answers (both parents and children).
- Arrange the children into groups. Each group goes to the assigned room with the group leaders. In the room, the children introduce themselves, and group leaders answer the children's questions, if they have any. The parenting class facilitator (or another program counselor) stays with the parents, further discusses with them group goals and possible influences, and answers their questions. [See Facilitator Note 5.]
- Children return to the main group, and the families leave. [See Facilitator Note 6.]

❑ General Considerations

PREVENTING NEGATIVE CONSEQUENCES OF GROUP ATTENDANCE FOR THE CHILDREN

As our research indicated, the group is perceived initially by most children as a serious, threatening place. Many of them do not come of their own free will but are "strongly prompted" to do so by their parents. Things negatively associated with group participation as reported by children and mothers include leaving school early, missing a favorite television show or a club activity, confronting the father's opposition to group, and facing the difficult issue of violence in the family.

An orientation for children and parents allows the children to become familiar with the agency and the program in a gradual and safe manner. Take all possible measures to avoid negative group-related consequences for the child by scheduling group after school hours and by seeking both parents' support and participation in the program whenever possible.

Support of the child's group participation by the nonreferring parent (who is often the abuser) is especially important for children who see this parent frequently. Such explicit support will prevent group participation from becoming another secret the child must keep in fear of a parent's reaction and may ease possible tensions in the child around issues of loyalty to the abusive parent. However, as mentioned in Chapter 3, involvement of the referring parent's partner or the child's other parent in the group should be pursued with extreme caution so as to not compromise the physical and emotional safety of the child and the victim/survivor.

KEEPING PARENTS INFORMED ABOUT GROUP

Several parents in our study felt frustrated and left out because they did not have satisfactory information about what their children were doing in the group. More specifically, this problem was related to confidentiality issues. Parents appeared to understand the purpose and benefits of the norm of confidentiality, but many of the mothers interviewed could not avoid feeling curious, uneasy, rejected, and out of control when their children chose not to share group experience with them. Confidentiality seemed to put a boundary between child and mother. Consider the following comments by one of the mothers:

> The hardest thing was that they told the kids that, you know, anything that was said there was to remain there. . . . That put me in a situation I've never been in before. Because if something's happened like say, between [my son] and his brother, and this one's saying this and this one's saying that . . . I need to know who started it or what actually is going on. And I couldn't do that with [my son]. I had no idea what he talked about . . . and that made me really uncomfortable. And I don't know if that's just being a mother or just that I know the information is real sensitive. But I didn't like that. (Mother of an 8-year-old boy, 2 months after group)

A discussion of group structure, contents, and norms in the orientation provides parents with the initial information they need to feel comfortable with their child's group participation. In this way, the orientation can prevent potential misunderstandings and frustrations caused by lack of sufficient information. Obviously, further and more detailed communication with parents regarding group activities and their potential effect on the child needs to be carried all through the 10 group sessions.

Children need to understand that they can talk with their parents about their personal group experiences, but not about what other children did or said in group.

NO-SHOW

It is our experience that the rate of no-shows for group participants in a community-based agency is relatively high. Many of the children assigned to group after the intake end up not showing on the first group session for a variety of reasons. The orientation enables the group leaders to test the commitment of candidate families to the group before the group starts and to take the necessary steps to ensure that the group will start with enough participants.

Box 4.4: Introduction of Group Goals

We would like to do many things with you in this group. As we said before, all of the children in these groups come from families in which parents fight. In the groups, we talk some about what happens to children when their parents fight. This may not always be easy, but we have learned from other children that after talking about it in the group, many of them felt better about themselves and their families.

It is very important for us to help you feel good about yourselves. We want you to feel strong and safe, and we talk about ways that can help you feel this way. And we also have fun; we have snacks, and sometimes we play.

❏ Facilitator Notes and Food for Thought

1. PRESENTATION OF GROUP GOALS

As the first step in trying to break the secret of violence, it is important that the children be aware from the very beginning that the group is centered on domestic violence, that all of the children who participate in the group come from families in which parents fight (or fought), and that we know about what happened in their families. Hence, it is important to introduce all four goals of the group, starting with breaking the secret. It is our experience that when children start off by perceiving the group as mostly a social and fun gathering, it is later very difficult to bring them to work on violence-related issues. Box 4.4 presents an example of an introduction of group goals to 7- to 9-year-old children.

2. ORIENTATION'S AUDIENCE

Keep in mind that both children and parents are your audience in the orientation, so use language and presentation style adequate for all ages. Both parents and children may have questions and concerns they would not like to raise in the presence of each other. Such concerns could be discussed when the children are taken by their group leaders to see the group room.

We sometimes use big puppets to present the group in the orientation. This seems to attract younger children and to be accepted with a smile by older children and parents.

3. ABSENCES AND BEING LATE FOR GROUP

Emphasize the importance of children's participation in each group session and of arriving on time. Children may have difficulties joining the group when they arrive late or after missing a previous session. We recommend that children who miss more than two sessions discontinue their participation in the current group and start in a new group at a later time.

4. ORIENTATION'S BOUNDARIES

The orientation is not a therapy or a parenting session, but aims primarily to provide information about the children's group. It is important that this be understood by parents and children and that you not allow the discussion to slide into personal issues that cannot be dealt with fully in this setting.

5. DISCUSSING GROUP INFLUENCES WITH PARENTS

The presentation of group goals to parents can follow the outline presented in Chapter 2 (Box 2.1 and Figure 2.1). It is important that parents understand not only the group goals and processes but also the potential influence on their children's behavior and on themselves. Parents need to be aware that group participation may create both healing and stressful effects stemming from group attendance, group activities and processes, and the achievement of group intended results (see Chapter 2 for more details). Specifically, parents need to be aware of the possible group effects listed in Box 4.5.

Help parents understand how these potentially problematic effects are an integral part of a healing process for the child. Reassure

---

Box 4.5: Possible Group Effects

- Children may talk about feelings and thoughts and ask questions regarding the violence they have not shared before with their parents. Discussing these issues may be emotionally stressful for the parents.
- Children may use new words and ideas they learned in group to define behaviors of people around them, including parents, as abusive or violent. This can be challenging to parents, who may feel criticized by their child.
- Children may display unusual or intensified behavior (e.g., acting out, withdrawal) after group sessions that were emotionally stressful for them.
- Children may behave in a more assertive way (or in what seems to them as assertive ways). For example, they might resist unwanted touch as part of trying to maintain safe personal space.

---

parents that they can turn to you with questions and concerns whenever the need arises during the group. Also, let the parents know that these issues will be discussed further in the parenting group.

6. TREATS

You may want to give a snack and a small present (e.g., a sticker, a balloon) to each of the children before they return to the main group.

Week One: Getting to Know Each Other

❏ **Message**

"It's okay to talk about abuse in group."

❏ Desired Outcomes for the Child

1. To feel comfortable with group leaders and other children
2. To understand the structure and main content of the program
3. To share some information about family
4. To learn that there are many types of families (e.g., single-parent, gay, divorced) and that all are normal
5. To be willing or to desire to come to the next group session

❏ Outline

Box 4.6: Outline for Session One

- Introductions: Introduce yourselves and then ask each child to say his or her name and why he or she is here. [See Facilitator Note 1.]
- Introduce the agency (agency's name, purpose, and clientele). You may start by asking the children to tell you what the name of the agency means.
- Introduce the program (structure of program and of each session, time table, general contents).
- Have "Getting to Know Each Other" Activities: [See Facilitator Note 2.].
- Group Rules and Discipline: Establish group rules (children and group leaders). [See Facilitator Note 3.]
- Family Drawing: Ask each child to draw a family member, the family home, and something the family likes to do together (one or more drawings, depending on time and concentration abilities of the children). [See Facilitator Note 4.]
- Children present drawings and group discusses varying family configurations and relationships.
- Check-In: Introduce check-in as part of each group session. Do check-in for today's group: "How did you feel about coming here, and how did you feel in the group today?" [See Facilitator Note 5.]
- Closure: "Pass the Squeeze"; Optional message: "It's okay to talk about abuse in the group." [See Facilitator Note 6.]

❏ General Considerations

ROOM SETTING

The group room should be hospitable for children. The space should be large enough to allow free play and some physical activity. We have found large floor cushions to be the most comfortable sitting arrangement. Minimal required furniture and equipment are floor cushions, table and chairs for drawing and writing activities, a chalkboard or easel board, paper, pencils and crayons, free-play toys, and accessories (including puppets). We also strongly recommend having a VCR in the group room.

SNACK

Children in our research talked about the snack as one of the most memorable aspects of group. The snack seemed to have contributed significantly to the children's positive and fun experience in the group. Some children are simply hungry after school, and most enjoy snacking anytime. The snack is also an opportunity for modeling egalitarian gender roles when both male and female group leaders prepare and serve the food.

We prefer nonsugared "health" snacks such as fruits, popcorn, and crackers with cheese or peanut butter. As a beverage, we prefer water or juice. To celebrate the last session, the children can be treated to their own choice of snack (e.g., ice cream, pizza).

The snack should be prepared and brought to the group room before the session starts. The decision about when to serve the snack depends on the session's agenda and on group dynamics. We usually serve the snack in the first half of the session and continue with the next activity while the children eat and drink.

BREAKING THE SECRET

"Breaking the secret" is a widely used metaphor for a common goal of intervention with victims of family violence. The phrase alludes not only to the tangible, solid nature of the emotional isolation that

Breaking the secret is a long, complex, and painful process.

many child witnesses of domestic violence appear to experience but also to the work required to deal with it. Breaking the secret is a long, complex, and painful process that involves the ability to identify and define violence, the awareness of feelings produced by the exposure to violence and its consequences, and the power to share with trusted others these feelings and the traumatic events that brought them about.

This process begins with the children's first visit to the domestic violence agency and continues throughout the group. The first group session is especially difficult for children because it forces them to face the existence of violence in their family in a group situation. Most children know that they are in the group because of the violence and that others know it as well. Consider the following quotes from our study:

> First I thought it was weird, because the first day I thought it was about the whole family doing abuse, and my mom said that it was about my dad drinking and stuff and doing stuff, but I thought it was for the whole family. . . . I never talked about my family [before]. . . . I was shy and stuff because I didn't want to be around people I didn't know. (9-year-old boy, 4 months after group)

> I thought [the group] would be like, you'd have to talk about every-thing that happened in the past. Anyway, I'm going like, "Oh no! Oh no! Oh no! There's no way I am telling my life, it's my personal stuff." (9-year-old girl, 1 month after group)

The main challenge of the first group session is to create a safe and comfortable atmosphere that encourages the children to come to the second group session willingly, while at the same time being clear that the group centers on children's experiences with violence at home. Children need to know that they will not be forced to share personal "stuff" and to believe that the group leaders and the other children will be able to handle the things they may wish to share.

❑ Facilitator Notes and Food for Thought

1. INTRODUCTIONS

Beginning the group by asking the children to say why they think they are here sends the children an important message. We let them know that they are in the group for a reason and not just for fun, that we plan to discuss violence-related issues in the group, and that we want them to talk about what happened in their families and can handle it.

2. "GETTING TO KNOW EACH OTHER" ACTIVITIES

Choose from the following list an activity that you like and that fits the developmental level and special circumstances of your group (e.g., a child with a physical disability, a majority of seemingly not very verbal children). Most of the suggested activities are appropriate for all ages. It might be better, however, not to challenge the younger children in the first session with an activity based on writing. It is most important that all children have a fair opportunity to introduce themselves through the chosen activity. Participate in the games if you are not needed as supervisor or facilitator of the activity.

Pay attention to the cultural appropriateness of the activity. For example, some cultures look negatively on saying good things about oneself, and so the activity "Affirmative Names" may not work with children from these ethnic groups.

Affirmative Names. In a circle, each player introduces him- or herself by giving one or two affirmative adjectives (characteristics). The adjectives can begin with the same letter as the player's first name (e.g., Marvelous Mary, Patient Paul). After everyone says his or her name, each player goes around the circle, trying to remember the names and adjectives of everyone else. The group helps players remember names when needed.

Three Things I Am Good At. Each player draws three things he or she is good at and pins it on the front of his or her shirt. Then everyone walks around the room to see the others' drawings and to show their own and talk about them.

Movement and Sound. Standing in a circle, each of the players introduces his or her name with a movement and a sound, and the entire group repeats after him or her. After all players have introduced themselves, the group goes around the circle doing the movement and the sound of each of the players. This game is more fun when the movements are exaggerated and the sounds are loud and clear.

In Common (for ages 7 and older). Everyone wanders around, finding out at least three things they have in common with each of the other players. These commonalities can be written down or just discussed. Provide the group with examples, such as hair color, height, number of siblings, hobbies, and birthdates.

Roller Ball. All players sit in a circle on the floor and spread out their legs so that each foot meets the foot of a neighbor. One player rolls a ball across the floor to be caught in someone else's legs. The "roller" calls out the other person's name. The "catcher" also can be asked a question, such as, "What is your favorite snack?" "What subject do you like most in school?" This game can be played also by tossing a soft ball or a bean bag from one player to another.

Decorate Your Name. Each person writes his or her name on a paper and decorates it with a design that expresses who he or she is. When finished, drawings are presented to the group.

Sharing Favorite Things. Pick several "things," such as food, color, animal, television show, movie, story, subject in school, or sport. Each person tells the group, or draws and then presents to the group, his or her favorite among these things.

Collage. Each person is given scissors, glue, posterboard, and magazines and is asked to create a collage about him- or herself. The collage can be directed to an area in the person's life, such as "what I like to do" or "my world." When finished, each person presents his or her work to the group. Make sure the magazines include pictures of all kinds of people: people of color, with disabilities, both genders, and so forth.

"Like" and "Don't Like" List. Each person writes a list of things he or she likes and doesn't like and presents it to the group. This can also be done orally.

Poem. Each person writes a poem about him- or herself and presents it to the group. The lines need not rhyme.

Box 4.7: Essential Rules for Group Participants

- Confidentiality (with the exception of suspicion of child abuse)
- No physical or verbal abuse or coercion
- Respect for others' opinions, feelings, and personal space (including listening while others talk)

Numbers. Each player picks a number between 1 and 10 and says it aloud. After everyone has chosen a number, the players are asked to say a number of things about themselves that equals the number they selected.

3. GROUP RULES AND DISCIPLINE

Group rules are a form of contract between the children and the group leaders and among the children. Rules allow clarity and predictability, basic components of a safe environment for children. Such an environment is especially important for child witnesses of domestic violence who have experienced emotional and physical threat or abuse. Rules need not be overemphasized; however, maintain as few rules as possible, and establish only realistic rules.

Children can suggest rules they would like to have in the group. This establishes the children's ownership of the group and thus empowers them. It is your responsibility, however, to ensure that certain essential rules are established and that inappropriate rules are not established. We consider the rules in Box 4.7 to be "essential rules."

Other rules suggested by the children can be added. However, rules that contradict the essential rules should not be accepted. Discuss unacceptable rules and help the children understand why these rules would not benefit the group. For example, a child in one of our groups suggested the rule "no talking without the permission of the teachers." We told her that this rule probably works well in school but that here in the group people may feel better if they can

Box 4.8: Suggestions for Effective Discipline

- Tell the child what to do, instead of what not to do.
- Avoid power struggles. Ask questions, rather than make statements.
- Let your tone of voice and posture do part of the work; bend to the child's height and speak softly.
- Keep your suggestions and directions to a minimum.
- Criticize the behavior, not the child.
- Redirect undesirable behavior.
- Look for creative solutions.

talk when they think they have something important to say and if it does not interfere with someone else talking.

Group rules can be written on a colorful poster to serve both as a constant reminder and as a decoration of the group room. Children can sign their names on the rules poster. This both empowers the children and helps establish the contractual nature of the rules. If you suspect that some group participants may be hard to discipline, you may want to make an individual "rules contract" with each child.

Once rules are established, it is your responsibility to enforce them. It is extremely important that group rules be enforced consistently and assertively from the beginning. Remember that groups need a balance of both intimacy and authority in order to work. Rule enforcement is a crucial factor in your ability to work with children who tend to act out. Your response to rule violations is a modeling opportunity for positive and constructive (rather than punitive and abusive) discipline. Effective discipline is a shared problem-solving process, rather than an adversarial confrontation. The suggestions in Box 4.8 may be helpful to keep in mind.

A common example of a rule violation that can be very disruptive for the group is when a child does not listen to what another child is saying as part of a group activity but instead distracts other children by teasing or talking with them. Box 4.9 shows examples of good and poor rule enforcement efforts in such a case.

Box 4.9: Examples of Rule Enforcement in Group

Setting: The group (10- to 12-year-olds) sits in a circle; children present family drawings they made. Rachel shows her drawing and starts to name her family members. Steve tries to draw with a crayon on Mike's leg. Mike chuckles, pulls his leg away, and tells Steve to stop. Steve tries again.

An example of poor rule enforcement:

Group Leader Steve, stop it! You seem not to care much about getting to know Rachel's family. Please put the crayon in the box and listen.

Steve (keeps the crayon) Okay, I will stop.

Group Leader (in a stern tone) I asked you to put the crayon back in the box. Please do it so we can continue.

Steve (raises his voice a little) Why do you care if I keep it? I don't do anything with it!

Group Leader You've heard what I said! One of the rules in this group is to respect each other, and you were disrespectful to Rachel. Come on, let's get it done with.

Steve I wasn't! I was just holding this crayon. I need to go to the bathroom. (gets up and leaves the room)

An example of good rule enforcement:

Group Leader Steve, Rachel is telling us about her family now. Maybe you want to draw on a paper while you listen?

Steve Okay. (doodles for a while and then rolls the paper into a tube and sticks it in Mike's arm)

Group Leader Steve, one of our rules here is to listen respectfully to each other. When you tease Mike, it is hard for Rachel to talk and for us to listen. Would you like a little break outside to help you get more relaxed?

Steve No, I don't wanna go outside.

Group Leader Okay, you don't have to, but then it means that you listen to Rachel, and once she is done, we will want to hear about your family too.

4. FAMILY DRAWING

Child witnesses of violence are a part of a variety of family compositions and living arrangements. We believe that all family configurations are legitimate and normal, and we deliver this message to the children while they draw and present their families. It is hard enough for children to deal with violence-related problems in their family; they need not feel that anything is wrong with their family composition as well.

Some children may find drawing difficult. Children often say that their picture is "no good" and that they cannot draw their family "the right way." Let children know there is no right or wrong way to draw and that any picture they produce is considered good. This includes symbolic representations of family members and the inclusion or exclusion of any family member from the drawing. When children present their pictures, ask them clarifying and supporting questions (e.g., "You drew a nice, smiling family, Annette; what kinds of things do you like to do for fun?" "Joel, you said you have three sisters, but I see only one in the picture").

Give children the option to talk about their families without showing their drawings to the group and let the children know they have the right not to share information with which they are uncomfortable. For example, if Joel responds to the above probe by blushing, lowering his eyes, and mumbling something, you can reassure him: "It's okay not to tell us why you chose not to draw your sisters. It seems like a difficult thing for you to do now."

5. CHECK-IN

The purpose of check-in is to allow children to talk about how they feel and to legitimate these feelings. Check-in also helps children identify and name feelings. In this session, check-in is introduced at the end of the meeting and is limited to a discussion of children's feelings about the first session. For all other sessions, check-in takes place at the beginning and centers on how the children felt during the last week and on the day of the group.

When children identify a feeling, encourage them to say why they are feeling the way they do. Box 4.10 presents an example.

Box 4.10: An Example of Check-In Dialogue

Group Leader Well, Mike. How did it feel coming here today?
Mike Okay.
Group Leader Can you say more about how you felt?
Mike It wasn't the greatest thing.
Group Leader Yeah, for most of the children who come here, it's not very easy the first time. Do you know why you weren't so excited about coming here?
Mike Because I couldn't go to my soccer game.
Group Leader Yeah, it can be annoying to miss a game. How do you feel now, after the group today?
Mike Okay, I suppose.
Group Leader Ahhmm . . .
Mike It's okay. It's not really like school.

It is important to allow each child adequate time and group attention when checking in. At the same time, check-in should not be extended beyond reasonable time limits or turn into the session's main focus. Make exceptions when children need to share and work on recent traumatic events, such as an eruption of violence at home.

Check-in can be done in a variety of ways:

Direct expression of feelings and thoughts. Older children may find it easier to discuss "highs" and "lows" of the previous week.

Feeling poster. Children choose a feeling (or feelings) from a poster or wall hanging that displays names of a variety of feelings. They explain their choices to the group.

Weather report. Children choose, from a poster describing several weather conditions, the one that reflects their feeling (e.g., sunny, foggy, cloudy, stormy) and explain to the group why they feel this way.

"If I were an animal." Children choose (with or without the help of an "animal poster") an animal with which they can identify or that they feel like. They explain their choices.

Feeling cards. (For older children) Each child gets 10 strips of construction paper (each about 0.5 in. × 4 in.). About 20 construction paper cards and some markers are set in the middle of the circle. The first child is asked to write on separate cards the different feelings he or she felt, put them face up in the center of the circle, and divide his or her paper strips among them so that the strongest feeling gets the most paper strips and the weakest one gets the fewest. The next child can use the same cards and add cards with new feelings. The check-in ends when all children have laid all their paper strips on feeling cards.

6. PASS THE SQUEEZE GAME

The Pass the Squeeze game is a closure "ritual" that brings the group together and gives the children an opportunity to hear the main message of the group and to express what they have learned that day. The children and the group leaders stand and hold hands in a circle, and a message is passed from one person to the next by saying it and squeezing the hand of the next person in the circle. Then the "squeezed" person says the message and squeezes the hand of his or her other neighbor, and so on around the circle.

You can suggest a message that reflects the main issue dealt with in the session. This activity also can be an opportunity to empower the children by letting them suggest their own message or by helping them construct one that is meaningful and that relates to the group content. It is our experience that even very young children can come up with good messages after a few sessions in which group leaders model the choice of a message.

With preadolescents, this activity may raise a problem when boys and girls do not want to hold each other's hands. We try to respect the children's wishes and suggest that the uncomfortable feeling may pass after the children get to know each other better. The activity also can be done either without holding hands or by passing an object from one child to the other while saying the message. Also, older children may think the game is a childish activity. In this case, you may want to replace it with another, more "mature," closing ritual. For example, children can say, in turn, what they learned today in group.

There is a difference between a child's ability to verbalize the group's message and his or her emotional internalization and acceptance of it. We found in our study that most children remember the main group messages, such as "It's okay to talk about abuse," "Abuse is not okay," and "The violence is not my fault." However, variables such as the children's personalities and developmental stage, family situations, and family histories of abuse may influence the children's readiness to incorporate these statements into their cognitive and emotional makeup.

Week Two: What Is Abuse?

❑ **Message**

"Abuse is not okay."

❑ **Desired Outcomes for the Child**

1. To become familiar with group participants, structure, and rules
2. To participate in activities about domestic violence
3. To learn that abuse is not okay under any circumstances
4. To learn basic definitions of violence and abuse

❑ **Outline**

Box 4.11: Outline for Session Two

- A name game (for a choice of activity, see Session 1, Facilitator Note 2).
- Check-in (for a choice of activity, see Session 1, Facilitator Note 5).
- Feeling of the day: sad. [See Facilitator Note 1.]
- Review group rules.
- "What is abuse?": Define violence and abuse and talk about their different forms. This can be done by brainstorming different ways of being abusive, with puppets who present scenes of abuse (especially effective for explaining emotional abuse), or with visual aids such as pictures of abusive behaviors the children have to identify. [See Facilitator Note 2.]
- Children draw an "Abuse is not okay" or "What hands can do" poster. [See Facilitator Note 3.]
- Closure: Personal affirmation. [See Facilitator Note 4.] "Pass the Squeeze"; Optional message: "Abuse is not okay."

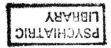

❏ General Considerations

LEARNING ABOUT ABUSE

By learning to define abuse, children construct a "violence vocabulary" that allows them to talk about abuse, share abusive experiences, and assign responsibility for abusive behavior. This information also enables them to learn that abuse is not okay and that it is not their fault when their parents fight.

Our research interviews and observations suggest that most, if not all, children can define abuse, distinguish among forms of abuse, and state that "abuse is not okay" at the end of the group and later on. However, it appears that although children know that abuse is wrong, parents sometimes think that their children do not apply this knowledge to their own behavior.

The process of defining interactions as abusive also can cause unintended stress for family members. Several mothers reported that their behavior was criticized by their children, who used the new information gained in the group. In the light of new knowledge acquired in the group, children may reevaluate their parents' behavior and parenting style. This appraisal occasionally has put parents in uncomfortable and even stressful positions. For example, a mother recalled the following:

> I guess she got into the aspects of the idea, of the abuse. The whole idea about abuse, and how people couldn't be abusive any more. . . . And in another sense she kind of used it too, to her advantage, by making statements. . . . She would say things like, "Well, if you touch me, I'll turn you in for child abuse!" . . . I felt like there were times when she has gotten, when she used it a lot. . . . I sometimes, I don't know if [the group] was good or bad. (Mother of a 9-year-old girl, 4 months after group)

Uncomfortable feedback by the child also, at times, had a potentially positive secondary impact on the parent:

> [My son] has occasionally told me if I was hollering, 'cause hollering was a big pattern in my family too, screaming and hollering and carrying on like that. And I really tried to cut down, but it, ya' know,

that's gonna take me time too, but he said, ya' know, "You're being abusive" and he does use this word which annoyed me at first, but I will usually stop and think about what he's saying to me. (Mother of a 10-year-old boy, 2 months after group)

Such feedback, coming from the child, can serve as reinforcement for a parent going through a change process aimed at nonabusive interaction patterns. This might especially be the case with parents who have completed groups for abusers or victims/survivors. Parents who have not gone through groups themselves may find "anti-abusive" responses of their child to be threatening, even to the point of further violence. Thus it is important to discuss this possible effect of the group with the parents during orientation and during the parenting group.

❑ Facilitator Notes and Food for Thought

1. FEELING OF THE DAY (SAD)

This activity is part of the group's "feeling education," which continually reaffirms the legitimacy of all feelings and their appropriate expression. Its aim is to strengthen children's awareness of different feelings, to help them label feelings, and to allow them to express different feelings. In all but the first and last sessions, you will focus on and discuss one feeling, usually at the beginning of the session after check-in. Most of the feelings discussed are relevant to the session's main theme. These feelings are (in order of sessions): sad, angry, ashamed/guilty, brave, hurt, afraid, strong, and happy.

Briefly present and discuss the "feeling of the day": sad. Visual aids such as drawings or puppets can be used for this purpose. For example, you can show posters illustrating scenes such as children saying good-bye to a parent who holds a suitcase and then ask the children what they think the children and the parent in the picture feel. A puppet can present the feeling of the day by saying in a crying voice that it is was very sad this week because it did not get a role in the school play.

After the initial presentation of the feeling, each child and group leader tells the group about a time in the last week when he or she felt this way. Sometimes it is difficult for children to remember a recent occasion; in that case, they can choose any relevant occasion they remember. Help the children understand better how they felt and what triggered the feeling and to connect the feeling with behavior (e.g., "What did you do when you felt sad?").

2. DEFINING ABUSE

People in all age groups tend to define a behavior by giving examples of it. We suggest that you include in the discussion of the different kinds of abuse—physical, sexual, and emotional—a general definition of abuse. *Abuse* can be defined as any behavior that physically or emotionally hurts another person and that is not an accident. Also discuss feelings that result from being abused and from abusing, such as fear, guilt, and feeling bad about oneself.

Emotional abuse is often more subtle than physical abuse and harder to identify. It is also a form of abuse that often is normalized and minimized. A definition of *emotional abuse* that can be used with children is "when one person makes another person feel really bad about him- or herself, and not by accident." Help children understand emotional abuse by giving them examples they can relate to, such as bullying behavior in school or putdowns by siblings. Then discuss how similar behaviors can occur between adults. The term *emotional abuse* can be replaced with *feeling abuse* for younger children.

> *Emotional abuse is often normalized and minimized.*

3. POSTER DRAWING

This activity combines an educational message with an opportunity for creativity. The completed posters also can serve as decorations for the group room or for the agency. Choose a topic for the poster and present it to the children. We suggest the topics "Abuse is not okay" or "What hands can do." Offer the children paper, crayons, markers, and pencils to use.

Abuse Is Not Okay!

Figure 4.1.

Abuse Is Not Okay! You may want to instruct the children to draw a "no-entrance" traffic sign and, within it, a picture of abuse. Or you can give them a prepared poster design to work with (see Figure 4.1).

Figure 4.2. What Hands Can Do

What Hands Can Do. Instruct the children to trace both of their hands on paper. Ask them to think about how hands can help or hurt, to write their thoughts around each of the hands, and then to decorate them (see Figure 4.2). This activity also can be done as a group collage/drawing with a large drawing of two hands.

4. POSITIVE AFFIRMATION

One of the main goals of the group is to strengthen children's self-esteem. Positive affirmation contributes directly to the achievement of this goal by providing children with an opportunity to acknowledge and share with others something positive about themselves. In this activity, the group stands in a circle and the children, in turn, describe a positive trait or something they are good at or one way in which they felt good about themselves in the past week.

Although it appears to be a simple exercise, it is our experience that many children find this activity very difficult. Some children are not used to being complimented, or even to thinking positively about themselves. Others will need your help in differentiating between participation in an enjoyable activity and appreciating an enjoyable trait in themselves (e.g., "I like playing football" vs. "I am good at football"). Still, it is important to insist on helping each child find a personal positive affirmation each week. For example:

> I think that it was good that they have these, like, positive affirmations. . . . It's something you like about yourself or someone said nice to you or something like that. (A 9-year-old boy, 4 months after group)

Week Three: Anger

❑ Message

"It's okay to be angry and express it, but it is not okay to abuse others with my anger."

❑ Desired Outcomes for the Child

1. To learn that all feelings, including "bad" ones, need to be acknowledged and felt
2. To know it is okay to express all feelings in group
3. To recognize one's own expressions of anger
4. To learn to differentiate between appropriate and inappropriate expressions of anger

❏ **Outline**

Box 4.12: Outline of Session Three

- Check-in.
- Feeling of the day: angry. [See Facilitator Note 1.]
- A story or a film and a discussion. [See Facilitator Note 2.]

Timm, S. A. (1981). *The dragon and the mouse.* Fargo, ND: Touchstone. (For all ages). A story about a big, powerful dragon and a small mouse who live together in a cave. The dragon uses his size and power to get the mouse to do what he wants him do to. The mouse is afraid of the dragon and mad at him. The story tells how the dragon learns to respect the mouse.

Discussion: Who had more power—the dragon or the mouse? How did the dragon and the mouse express their anger? Were they abusive? How did the dragon try to control the mouse? How did the mouse feel when the dragon tried to control him? Did you ever feel or behave like the dragon or like the mouse? What were other feelings the dragon and the mouse felt for each other? Can people love and be angry at one another at the same time?

Preston, E. M. (1976). *The temper tantrum book.* New York: Puffin. (Ages 4 to 6). A story about various animals that are angry and ways they express their anger.

Discussion: Do you ever get mad like the animals in the story? What do you do when you get mad? How does your body feel when you get mad? What are some other feelings you have when you get mad? Who is a safe person to talk with when you get mad?

Simon, N. (1974). *I was so mad.* Niles, IL: Albert Whitman. (Ages 4 to 9). A story about various situations that make children mad. The story validates children's feelings of anger.

(continued)

Box 4.12: Continued

Discussion: What are some things you get mad about? Did you ever feel like the child in the story? What do you do when you get angry? Is it okay to hit, yell, kick, and break others' toys? What else can you do when you get angry? What are some other feelings you have when you get mad? Who is a safe person to talk with when you get mad? How does your body feel when you get mad?

Berry, J. (Producer). *The value of properly handling emotions* [Film from the series "Human Race Club Kids teach values."] (24 min.). (#5604-V). Distributed by KIDSRIGHTS. (Ages 7 to 9; only first 15 minutes are recommended.) For further information, call 1-800-892-KIDS or (904) 483-1100.

Club members recall an argument about who would drive the club's lean mean machine in town. Members learn that not handling uncomfortable emotions properly results in problems.

Discussion: Do you get mad at your friends like Maggie? What do you do when you get mad? Is it okay to feel angry? Is it okay to hurt others when you are mad at them? Is it okay to hurt yourself? What else can be done?

- "Personal expression of anger" exercise:
  Younger children: Ask children to act out, in turn, their typical behavior/response when they are angry (e.g., "What do you do when you are angry?" "How do you look when you are angry?"). The acting is followed by a discussion of personal and general appropriate and inappropriate expressions of anger. [See Facilitator Note 3.]
  Older children: Children draw a picture or make a sculpture with clay that represents how they feel when they are angry. Discuss personal and general appropriate and inappropriate expressions of anger.
- Free play [See Facilitator Note 4] or free-time activity. [See Facilitator Note 5.]
- Closure: Personal affirmation. "Pass the Squeeze"; Optional message: "It's okay to be angry but not to abuse others with my anger."

❏ **Facilitator Notes and Food for Thought**

1. FEELING OF THE DAY (ANGRY)

Anger is usually the most familiar feeling for child witnesses of domestic violence. Often it is a secondary feeling that masks other feelings, such as shame, fear, and pain. It is also a feeling connected most immediately with the eruption of violence. This is why we chose to devote an entire session for exploring anger.

2. STORIES

Young children usually love to be told stories. Older children, however, may think it a childish activity. In this case, you can let the children participate in reading a story by passing the book around the circle and letting each child read a page. You may want to guide the children's listening by asking them to pay attention to certain issues in the story, such as the suggested discussion questions.

3. PERSONAL EXPRESSION OF ANGER

This activity has two purposes: (a) to help children recognize their own appropriate and inappropriate ways of expressing anger and, if needed, (b) to teach them alternative behaviors. Appropriate ways of expressing anger are those that do not involve the abuse of self, other people, animals, or property. Davis (1984), in her book *Something Is Wrong at My House*, suggests: "I can get rid of some of the mad feelings in me without being mean. I feel better when I run, dance, jump rope, play my drums, draw a picture, write a story or make up a song" (p. 18).

Some professionals suggest that hitting a pillow or another unbreakable object is a legitimate and therapeutic way of releasing anger. We oppose this view. Hitting an object is closely associated with abuse. It can serve as a modeling of physical violence and can constitute a threat in and of itself. The message we want to convey to children is that hitting is wrong in any shape or form.

Some children, especially preadolescent boys, may use different violent behaviors to express their anger, thus becoming both victims and perpetrators of violence. Such behaviors can include torturing animals, bullying other children, vandalism, and hitting their siblings or parents. In some extreme cases, you may want to refer the child to a young perpetrators group or to individual therapy around these issues.

4. FREE PLAY

Free play can serve as a release of tension accumulated during the session. Children's free play is influenced by the availability of time, space, toys, and props. Observations of children's free play and interactions with one another can provide group leaders with an opportunity to gather additional information on the children.

Have props (e.g., clothes, hats, handbags, shoes, jewelry, scarves, gloves, pillows) and toys (e.g., cars, dolls, dollhouse, soft balls, sand table, Legos, puppets) available for the children to play with. Also have art supplies available for the children to create with (e.g., paper of different sizes and colors, magazines, markers, crayons, colored pencils, tape, glue, stapler, scissors, modeling clay, chalk).

You may want to keep these props and supplies away from children's eyes and hands during the rest of the session. The presence of such materials in the group room is likely to distract children from group activities and to become a constant source of friction between children and group leaders.

5. FREE-TIME ACTIVITIES

Free-time activities are meant to give children a break from the regular activities of the group and, when needed, to allow them to relax and release tension accumulated in other activities. Allow yourself the flexibility to alter a predecided free-time activity, depending on the needs of the group. For example, when children seem tense or act out, you may want to choose a relaxation exercise; however, when children seem uneasy after a long "sitting" activity, you may want to choose a movement game, such as "shaking."

All of the following activities fit all ages, unless an age is specified. You may find, however, that some older children are reluctant to participate in movement games, considering them to be "stupid" and "childish."

Instant Relaxation. This exercise can be done sitting, standing, or lying down.*

INSTRUCTIONS

Let's close our eyes.

Now tense every muscle in your body at the same time. Legs, arms, jaws, fists, face, shoulders, stomach. Hold them ... tightly. Now relax and feel the tension pour out of your body. Let all of the tension flow out of your body and your mind, replacing the tightness with calm, peaceful energy, letting each breath you take bring calmness and relaxation into your body.

Pause

Now tense your body again and hold it for a few seconds. Then let go, relaxing and feeling all of the tension flow out of your body.

Pause

And now tense every muscle in your body and at the same time take a deep breath for a few seconds. Then say to yourself "relax," and when you do, let your breath go and relax.

Pause

Take a deep breath and hold it about 10 seconds. Then say to yourself "relax" and let yourself go.

Pause

When you feel like relaxing, just take a deep breath, hold it for a few seconds, say to yourself "relax," and let it go. You can do this wherever you are because nobody can hear you or see you. Practice this again by yourself two or three times.

Pause

Now open your eyes slowly, feeling calm and alert.

The Stretch. This exercise can be done with music.*

INSTRUCTIONS

Let's all begin walking slowly around the room, getting the feeling of our bodies in motion. Feel the way we move, the way our feet contact the floor. As you walk, begin to raise your arms, stretching as high as you can on each step . . . feeling yourself stretch from your toes to your fingers.
Pause (1 minute)
And now with each slow step, stretch from side to side, bending like a tree in the wind.
Pause (30 seconds)
Now bend forward and walk with your arms hanging loosely, almost to the floor.
Pause (30 seconds)
And now take slow, giant steps, stretching your legs.
Pause (30 seconds)
And now, once more, stretch up to reach to the sky.
Pause (10 seconds)
And now stand still and feel good.

Shaking. This exercise is easy. Each child finds a comfortable spot in the room and then just shakes his or her whole body. The exercise can be done with music and with colorful scarves or crepe paper tied to the children's wrists. It can be done gradually, with instructions from the group leader to shake different body parts.*

Pretending We Are Balloons. Children stand up and spread around the room so that each has enough space to move around. Together with the group leader, everyone inhales and expands like a balloon. When the "balloon" cannot take in anymore air, it empties out, slowly falls to the floor, and shrinks into a limp piece of rubber. Add

* From *The Centering Book: Awareness Activities for Children and Adults to Relax the Body and Mind,* by G. Hendricks and R. Wills. Englewood Cliffs, NJ: Prentice Hall. Copyright © 1975 by Prentice Hall/a Division of Simon & Schuster, Englewood Cliffs, NJ. Reprinted with permission.

"balloon sound effects" for both expanding and shrinking. This exercise can be repeated several times.

Dancing With Scarves. Put colorful, light scarves in the center of the room. Play music and encourage the children to choose a scarf and dance with it. Remind them to be careful not to bump into each other while dancing. In harmony with the music, children can pretend they are on the moon, on a tropical island, or elsewhere.

Clowns. Children pretend they are clowns moving their whole body to make people laugh. The clowns can show any emotion: They can be silly, mean, sad, funny, tricky, and so forth.

Machine. Everyone stands in a circle. One person goes to the middle of the circle and starts a motion and a sound. The other players take turns "attaching" themselves to the machine, adding a motion and a sound of their own.

Emotional Statues. Everyone is given a note with the name of a feeling written on it. Taking turns around the circle, each person makes him- or herself into a statue, portraying the feeling. Other group members guess the feeling.

Doodle Drawing. Ask the children to draw doodles, abstract images, and shapes. Then ask them to find a picture in the lines and shapes they created. The pictures can be outlined, colored, or otherwise emphasized.

Group Mural. The group leader or the children decide on a theme for a mural—for example, "Things I like to do," "Things that I am good at," "What hands can do," "My wish." The theme could relate to the group message or the feeling of the day. The mural can be created on a chalkboard or grease board with markers, or on cardboard with various techniques. Make sure that each child has a chance to contribute to the group mural.

Make Believe (Zimmerman, 1987). The group leader asks "make believe" questions. All children have an opportunity to answer while the others listen. Children also can make up their own questions. Responses can be graphic, rather than oral. Here are examples of questions:

> Make believe rainbows were handed to you. What would you do with them, and how would you feel?
>
> Make believe it rained music instead of water. What kinds of things would grow?
>
> Make believe that once a year you could change yourself into any kind of creature. What would you become?
>
> Make believe you could throw the most fun party in the world. Where would it be? Whom would you invite? What would you do?
>
> Make believe you could dream any dream you wanted. What would you dream about?
>
> Make believe you had a net to catch a favorite moment in your life. Which would it be?
>
> Make believe someone gave you a golden treasure box. What would you place in it? Or hope to find inside?
>
> Make believe you could ask a bird to deliver a special message. What would it say, and to whom would you send it?
>
> Make believe you could wave a magic wand. What two wishes would come true?

Telephone (Butler, 1986, p. 64). As players sit in a circle, someone whispers a message to the next person, who in turn repeats it to the next player, and so on around the circle. Each player whispers the message only once. After the message has completed the circuit, the last person repeats it aloud for comparison with the original message. Two messages can be sent at once, one to the right and another to the left.

Alphabetical Sentence (Butler, 1986, p. 60) (Ages 7 to 12). The first player starts a sentence by saying a word beginning with *a*. The next person adds a second word beginning with *b*. The sentence continues, each player adding a word, until a long sentence has been created using the whole alphabet as the first letters of the words. If a dead end is reached, a player may begin a new sentence with the next alphabetical letter.

Week Four: When Parents Fight

❏ **Message**

"It's not my fault when someone is abusive to me and when other people abuse each other."

❏ **Desired Outcomes for the Child**

1. To know that no one deserves abuse and that domestic violence is never the children's fault
2. To share some personal experience related to violence at home
3. To differentiate between a person and his or her behavior; knowing that it is possible and okay to love a parent while condemning his or her violent behavior
4. To learn that people are responsible for their behavior and can change it

❏ **Outline**

Box 4.13: Outline for Session Four

- Check-in.
- Feeling of the day (one of the following, depending on the children's ages and level of understanding: feeling mixed up, confused, ashamed, guilty. [See Facilitator Note 1.]
- Story or a film. [See Facilitator Note 2.]

Bernstein, S. C. (1991). *A family that fights*. Morton Grove, IL: Albert Whitman. (All ages)

Davis, D. (1984). *Something is wrong in my house: A book about parents fighting*. Seattle: Parenting Press. (All ages)

Otto, M. (1988). *Never, no matter what*. Toronto: Women Press. (All ages; suitable for shelter groups)

(continued)

Box 4.13: Continued

Paris, S. (1985). *Mommy and daddy are fighting.* Seattle: Seal Press. (Ages 4 to 8)

All four books describe families in which the mother is being abused by the father, with an emphasis on how the abuse influences the children.

Trudeau, P. M. (Producer). *Enfantillage—Kidstuff* [Film]. (6 min.). Distributed by: National Film Board of Canada, P.O. Box 6100, Station "A," Montreal, Quebec H3C 3H5, Canada.

Intense and powerful, this short film combines drawings and puppet animation to convey how violence at home tears at the equilibrium and sensitivity of a child.

Benerjee Associates (Producers). *Secret wounds: Working with child observers of family violence* (Part II) [Film]. (8 vignettes, 1-4 min. each). Distributed by: Benerjee Associates, 178 Tamarack Circle, Dept. B, Skillman, NJ 08558. (609) 683-1261.

Animated vignettes based on drawings by child witnesses of woman battering. The children's voices are heard discussing their experiences.

- Discuss the story or film and related personal experiences of the children. Ask: What does it feel like when parents fight? Who is responsible for the fighting and abuse? What can parents do about the fighting? What can children do when parents fight? Is it possible to feel both love and hate or anger toward a parent? [See Facilitator Note 3.]
- Free play or free-time activity (for a choice of activity, see Session 2, Facilitator Notes 4 and 5)
- Optional: (a) Describe and/or act out short scenarios that involve abusive interactions; ask the children to identify who is responsible for the abuse. (b) Brainstorm with the children what children worry about when their parents fight.
- Closure: Personal affirmation. "Pass the Squeeze"; Optional message: "Abuse is not my fault."

❏ General Considerations

SHARING PERSONAL EXPERIENCE

By the fourth session, some children feel safe enough to open up and share with the group some of their personal experiences of violence at home. Others still find it difficult. Be tuned into and respect the individual pace of each child. Do not push the ones who do not want to share, and support and encourage the ones who do.

Sharing personal experiences with the group simultaneously reduces and increases stress for the children. Talking about violence that occurred in their homes requires children to remember what happened, to peel away layers of defenses they have constructed over time. To share is to remember, and remembering has its costs. Consider the following quote from our study:

> [In the group] they would help you forget what happened and try to make you happy. . . . But first remember what you did and then forget. . . . First I forgot all about [it] and then I watched the movie and I remembered that my dad threw a pot, and then, that's in my mind; so I can't get it out of my head any more. They made me remember 'cause of that bad movie. . . . They gave me back my memory about it, and I wasn't so glad about it. (A 7-year-old girl, 1 month after group)

Another girl eloquently described the stress involved in talking about the violence experienced:

> I sort of get, I get this picture in my head, and it just all goes black. And then I get teary eyes, but I don't cry. That is pretty new. And then my stomach starts to hurt. . . . I think like from talking about it all the time I just, I just get one thing in my head, and then another thing, and then another thing. And so my mind, my mind isn't all that big, you know. It can only fit so many things and, so it just gets all black. And then it just, some of it goes to my eyes and gets all teary. But I don't cry for some reason. And then my stomach hurts, probably 'cause I'm nervous. . . . 'Cause it's from talking about this stuff so much from DAP, probably. . . . I don't really know what to think of it. It's just, it's definitely not normal. 'Cause I wouldn't think that would happen to any other kid. (An 8-year-old girl, 1 month after group)

Although talking about family violence is stressful for children, children have some capacity to protect themselves from being overwhelmed by such stress. In our study, we found children to be selective about what they chose to share with the group. Many of them seemed to have the ability to maintain safe boundaries in the group by controlling the amount and type of information they shared. For example:

> One of [the children], she had everything to say, well, she said just about everything. It's like she had nothing to hide or something like that. . . . I thought that if I was that person, I'd be quite embarrassed. . . . I told a little bit, some of it. Some things I just didn't really want to tell. Didn't feel like it. (A 9-year-old boy, 4 months after group)

Listening to their friends' stories, children discover they are not the only ones whose family experienced violence. This is especially meaningful for children who never have spoken openly about the violence in their homes and who feel ashamed, guilty, and confused about it. It is often a great relief to discover that what they thought was an extremely deviant family situation is actually shared with other families.

ABUSED CHILDREN

While sharing personal experiences of violence, listening to a story, or watching a movie, children appear to note not only the mere existence of violence in other homes but also its form, severity, and victims. Children compare the violence they have experienced with the violence experienced by others in their group, as demonstrated by the following quote:

> Some of those kids in my group really had to suffer a lot. . . . Their parents would abuse them. . . . A few of the kids, the only thing that happened was the dad pushing the mom. . . . And some of the pain, some of the pain that some of the kids in my group and their parents had to suffer. (A 9-year-old boy, 4 months after group)

Ironically, by realizing that "it can be worse," children can feel better about themselves and their families. This may be especially true when children who witnessed violence between their parents compare their circumstances with those of children who themselves were physically or sexually abused. Such comparisons, however, may have grave consequences for the abused child. This child may come to the conclusion that even in an environment where the secret of family violence is shared, he or she is nonetheless different in having still another shameful secret that is hard to share.

Our research data provided some support for this hypothesis. In the group we observed, only one child had been physically abused (by her father). Although she shared experiences with the group otherwise, she did not disclose this particular information throughout the 10 sessions. Only in the family session conducted with her mother was it finally disclosed.

You may want to consider the possibility of having separate groups for children who were also abused or, at a minimum, include more than one abused child when composing the group. As discussed in Chapter 2, children who have experienced and have not received treatment for long-standing emotional, physical, sexual, or ritualistic abuse directed at them need to work on their own abuse first, before participating in the program described in this manual. If abused children are included in the group, group processes that permit breaking the secret of child abuse must be incorporated into the program. For example, when discussing definitions of violence and abuse, include examples of abuse of both adults and children by another adult.

❏ Facilitator Notes and Food for Thought

1. DEVELOPMENTAL UNDERSTANDING OF FEELINGS

Kauffman (1980) suggests that although children's shame and guilt experiences feel bad, the capacity to translate those experiences into words and to link them into one's identity has not matured. It is our experience that younger children do not understand the meaning of the words *shame* and *guilt* but can relate to other feelings, such as *confusion* and *being mixed up* to describe situations that older children perceive as shame producing.

Hence, we encourage you to choose for the "feeling of the day" with younger groups any feelings that seem to tap into children's emotional experience of guilt and shame.

2. OBTAINING FILMS

The films we suggest for this and other sessions will make a great contribution to your program. However, we are aware that some agencies and shelters lack the resources to purchase these films. One solution for this problem is to ask a public library, university video library, or high school library in your area to purchase the films so that you can borrow them later. Another possibility is to apply for a grant or to hold a fund-raising event for purchasing video equipment and films for your children's program.

3. PARENTS' RESPONSIBILITY FOR THE VIOLENCE

Not all child witnesses of domestic violence take responsibility for the violence directed at their parents, but many of them do. One of the goals of this session is to help children know that the abuse at home is not their fault. Although the majority of battered women are victims of abusive partners, many children tend to blame their mother for the violence or to see her as having some responsibility for it. Teach the children that people are responsible for their violent behavior and that nothing, including what may seem to be a provocation, justifies abuse.

This teaching can be done by presenting and discussing different scenarios for a conflictual event, demonstrating that people choose their responses out of several possible ones and, hence, are responsible for their choices. Conflictual scenarios can be enacted with the help of puppets, role-played by the group leaders, or illustrated on posters. Box 4.14 presents an example of such an event.

In the process of defining abuse and talking about family violence, many of the children realize that their mother's partner, who is often their father, is the abuser and the one responsible for the violence. Attributing the responsibility for the violence to their

Give children permission to have contradictory feelings and conflicting loyalties.

Box 4.14: An Example of "Responsibility for Abuse" Exercise

Setting: A father and a very young girl are in the kitchen, eating breakfast. The little girl accidentally turns over her cup, and milk spills on the floor. She looks startled and as if she is about to cry.

Scenario A:

Father You stupid! Look what you did! Why can't you be more careful? Now get up and clean it.

Scenario B:

Father Oops, we have some milk on the floor. Nothing too bad happened. I'll get a rag, and you can wipe it up.

Questions for discussion: How did the little girl feel in each of the stories? How did the father feel in each of the stories? Could the father in the first story have changed how he felt about the accident? Could he have changed the way he talked to the girl? Did it happen to you before that you were angry but chose not to show it in a way that could hurt someone else?

father may weigh heavily on the children's shoulders. They may believe that their love for the abuser cannot coexist with their anger and frustration about the violent behavior. It is extremely important to give children permission to have contradictory feelings and conflicting loyalties—that is, to love BOTH the abuser and the victim; to love AND hate or be angry with their parents.

Week Five: It's Not Always Happy at My House

❏ **Messages**

"I'm not the only one whose parents fight."
"Abuse hurts."

❏ Desired Outcomes for the Child

1. To be aware of some of the feelings produced by the experience with violence (e.g., anger, pain, frustration, fear, confusion, guilt, sadness)
2. To know that other families experience violence

❏ Outline

Box 4.15: Outline for Session Five

- Check-in.
- Feeling of the day: brave. [See Facilitator Note 1.]
- Film. [See Facilitator Notes 2 and 3.]

It's not always happy at my house [Film]. (33 min.). (#5119M). Distributed by: MTI Film & Video, 108 Wilmont Rd., Deerfield, IL 60015 (800) 621-2131. (All ages)

The film traces the consequences of woman battering on three children in a family, leading to their admission to a battered women's shelter.

MacDonald, J. (Producer). *The crown prince* [Film]. (38 min.). National Film Board of Canada. Distributed by: The Media Guild, 11722 Sorrento Valley Rd., Suite E, San Diego, CA 92121 (619) 755-9191. (Ages 10 to 12)

The film depicts the feelings and frustrations of two sons of a battered woman: a grade-school child and an adolescent. The film explores issues related to student disclosure to a teacher.

Discuss the movie and the children's reactions to it. Integrate themes from previous group discussions, including definitions of abuse (especially physical and emotional), responsibility for the violence, self-protection, feelings and attitudes about violence; comparison between the children's own experience and that of the children in the movie; and feelings evoked by the movie.

- Closure: Personal affirmation. "Pass the Squeeze"; Optional messages: "I'm not the only one whose parents fight" and "Abuse hurts."

❑ Facilitator Notes and Food for Thought

1. FEELING OF THE DAY (BRAVE)

This session's feeling—brave—is an empowering one. A discussion of incidents in which the children felt brave will help prepare them to cope with the difficult feelings and memories that may be raised by the upcoming film. Although we want to help the children acknowledge and express painful feelings, it is just as important that we help them recognize their strengths and coping skills.

2. IF YOU CANNOT GET A FILM

The issues evoked by watching one of the recommended films are similar to those covered in previous sessions and in Session 6. The uniqueness of this session is in the emotional intensity created by the medium through which these issues are being processed—that of a well-made film. We are not aware of an alternative medium that can replace film and that is not included in other sessions. Hence, we recommend that program leaders who cannot get one of the films follow Session 4 with Session 6. In this case, however, you may want to consider replacing the feeling of the day in Session 6 (hurt) with that of Session 5 (brave).

3. FILM

The children in our study watched the film *It's Not Always Happy at My House*. For many of them, this was the most memorable group activity. The impact of the movie on the children was strong. For example:

> [My daughter] talked about seeing a movie, and she was quite relieved that her daddy had never hit me. . . . She had more to say about that than any of the other groups. . . . She was agitated. (Mother of an 8-year-old girl, 1 month after group)

Many children become agitated while watching the movie and stay emotionally vulnerable long after the group session is over. Several steps must be taken to ensure the children's emotional safety while

---

Box 4.16: Guidelines for Showing a Domestic Violence Film

- Inform parents about the content of the film and the child's potential reactions to it. If possible, allow parents to watch and discuss the film in the parenting group, either before the children watch it or at the same time. We recommend that children and parents do not see the movie together, to allow free expression of feelings and thoughts triggered by the film.
- Prepare the children by discussing with them the content of the film and some of their possible reactions to it (e.g., "We will see a movie today about children whose dad was abusive to their mom. Some children feel sad or angry when they see this movie. It's a pretty hard movie, and it's okay to feel like this. You can also close your eyes or leave the room if it gets too hard to watch the movie").
- Pay special attention to the children's emotional state at check-in and give them the time and attention they need to process any emotionally loaded issues before they watch the film.
- Be familiar with the film before you show it to the children. During the film, watch the children's reactions and, if necessary, give them verbal affirmation and support for their feelings. You might even stop the movie for a brief discussion if that seems appropriate.
- In the discussion following the film, allow each child to express feelings and thoughts provoked by the film.

---

they watch the movie in the group and also later at home. Guidelines that we suggest you follow are presented in Box 4.16.

Week Six: Sharing Personal Experiences With Violence

❏ **Messages**

"I'm not the only one whose parents fight."
"It's okay to tell the group about the violence in my family."

❏ Desired Outcomes for the Child

1. To share with the group personal and family experiences related to violence and to experience the accompanying feelings
2. To know that the other children in the group experience domestic abuse as well

❏ Outline

Box 4.17: Outline for Session Six

- Check-in.
- Feeling of the day: hurt. [See Facilitator Note 1.]
- Children draw a violent event (or a "scary fight") that has happened in their family. [See Facilitator Note 2.]
- Children present their drawings. Talk about the children's feelings at the time of the event and while doing the drawings.
- Free play or free-time activity (for a choice of activity, see Session 2, Facilitator Notes 4 and 5). [See Facilitator Note 3.]
- Closure: Personal affirmation. "Pass the Squeeze"; Optional message: "It's okay to tell the group about violence in my family."

❏ Facilitator Notes and Food for Thought

1. FEELING OF THE DAY (HURT)

Hurt as used here means both physical and emotional pain. Children more readily think of concrete examples of physical hurt. Encourage the children to acknowledge and discuss the more intangible incidents during which they felt emotionally hurt.

2. DRAWING A VIOLENT EVENT

Drawing and discussing a witnessed violent event allows children to examine some of their thoughts and feelings about the violence, to get support for them, and to learn about the witnessing experiences, feelings, and thoughts of other group members.

This activity can be very painful for children. Expressing feelings tied to traumatic experiences is a difficult and stressful experience in and of itself, even when it is legitimated and supported. The following observations from our study illustrate how emotionally loaded this activity can be:

[Group Leader (GL) A asks the children to draw the most violent event they either saw or heard in their family.]

Sharon Well, there was no violence in my family, nothing really happened.
GL A Was there any yelling or threatening?
Sharon Yeah.
GL A Well, you know, that's what you should draw.

[Sharon is getting agitated. She plays with her juice and makes all kinds of grimaces.]

Sharon (after a short while) Can I draw myself as an animal again?
GL A Sure.

[Sharon starts drawing an animal and, while drawing, groans and moans.]

Sharon I can't! I can't draw it. I can't do yelling.

[Sharon talks with GL A about drawing yelling and other alternatives. She keeps drawing for a while and then stops and puts her face on the floor. Then she raises her head again and continues to draw. She says she is frustrated because she can't draw a lion the way she would like. Then she turns her paper to the other side and starts a new picture.]

GL B You know, sometimes when we do things like that, it brings back all the feelings we felt when these things happened. That's fine. We know it's hard, but it's all right.

GL A Sometimes we feel sad or mad about the things that happened.

[The children continue to draw for a while. Amy tells GL A she doesn't feel very well and goes out to drink water. Then Sharon says she doesn't feel very well, stops drawing, hugs her stuffed giraffe, and lies down on the floor, curled like a baby with her giraffe. She is saying again that she doesn't feel very well, that she wasn't feeling well all the time, but that now she really doesn't feel well.] (Observations of seventh group session; children are 8- and 9-year-olds)

As illustrated in the above quote, children often deal with the bad feelings produced by this exercise by talking with peers, drawing other pictures, walking around the room, tearing up or scribbling on their pictures, or refusing to draw altogether. Support the children by affirming their difficulties. Encourage, but do not force, them to draw. Some children may be able to talk about but not draw the most violent event. Soft background music can create a pleasant atmosphere and help children concentrate on their drawings.

When the children present their drawings, support and encourage them, but do not push them to talk about what they are not ready to share with the group. Allow the children to talk about their pictures or the events they drew without showing the picture itself.

This session's focus on the family's most difficult moments can be distressing and even disempowering for the children. Although some of the pain cannot be avoided, you can help the children by reminding them of their parents' strength in coping with the violence (by looking for help and by working to prevent further incidents of abuse).

3. FREE PLAY OR FREE-TIME ACTIVITY

The purpose of this activity is to allow children to release some of the tension accumulated while drawing and talking about the violent events that happened in their families. Hence, do not choose a game that would demand much cognitive or emotional effort by the children.

Week Seven: Touch

❑ **Message**

"My body is private, and I have the right to protect it."

❑ **Desired Outcomes for the Child**

1. To learn to differentiate between appropriate and inappropriate touch
2. To know what to do in the event of attempted or actual sexual or physical abuse
3. To know that one's body is private and that one has the right not to share it if it feels uncomfortable
4. To accept fear as a legitimate and helpful emotion

❑ **Outline**

Box 4.18: Outline for Session Seven

- Check-in.
- Feeling of the day: afraid. [See Facilitator Note 1.]
- "Good touch-bad touch" exercise. [See Facilitator Note 2.]
- A story or film.

Girard, L. W. (1984). *My body is private.* Niles, IL: Albert Whitman. (Ages 4 to 9)

The story teaches children about the meaning of privacy, focusing specifically on the body. The main messages are that no one can touch children's bodies without their permission and that they should tell a trusted adult if someone violates their privacy.

(continued)

Box 4.18: Continued

Davis, N., & Custer, K. (1990). Little Bunny learns to say no. In N. Davis, *Once upon a time: Therapeutic stories to heal abused children* (rev. ed., pp. 43-46). Oxon Hill, MD: Psychological Associates of Oxon Hill. (Ages 4 to 9) [See Facilitator Note 3.]

Wachter, O. (1983). *No more secrets for me.* Boston: Little, Brown. (Ages 7 to 12)

The book presents four short stories about children who were touched in a way that didn't feel good and how they took care of themselves and got help from a trusted adult.

J. Gary Mitchell Film Company. (Producer). *What tadoo with fear* [Film]. (20 min.). (#5173M). Distributed by: MTI Film & Video, 108 Wilmont Rd., Deerfield, IL 60015 (800) 621-2131. (Ages 4 to 9)

This film explores, with the help of puppets, both the positive and negative aspects of fear. It also gives real-life examples of situations to show children how they can conquer fear and open up to adults they trust.

Media Ventures and The Illusion Theater. *Touch* [Film]. (33 min.). Distributed by: Media Ventures Video, 1458 W. Minnehaha Pkwy., Minneapolis, MN 55409. (Ages 7 to 12)

Screenplay adaptation of The Illusion Theater's play about sexual abuse prevention. Discusses nurturing, confusing, and exploitative touch and teaches prevention and safety skills.

Lanett, R., with Crane, B. (1985). *It's okay to say no! A parent/child manual for the protection of children.* New York: Tom Doherty. (Ages 4 to 9)

The book includes a series of short stories aimed at developing children's awareness of potential situations in which they may be victimized and of how they can protect themselves.

- Discuss the story or film: How do we know that a touch is a bad touch? What does our fear tell us? When do we call a bad touch sexual abuse? What can you do to protect yourself when someone touches you in a bad way? [See Facilitator Note 4.]
- Personal Space exercise. [See Facilitator Note 5.]
- Closure: Personal affirmation. "Pass the Squeeze"; Optional message: "My body is private, and I have the right to protect it."

❏ **General Considerations**

ABUSED CHILDREN

The aims of this session are to provide the children with basic definitions and an understanding of appropriate and inappropriate touch and to teach them basic protective skills. This session is not designed to be and is not sufficient as an intervention with children who were sexually or physically abused. Children you suspect or know have been abused should be referred to an agency or a clinician who deals specifically with child abuse.

Although self-disclosure of sexual or physical abuse is not encouraged in this session, be ready for the possibility that a child will disclose past or present abuse. If a child discloses abuse, acknowledge that you heard him or her (e.g., "I am sorry that it happened to you; it wasn't your fault") and arrange to get more details later (e.g., "I am interested in hearing more about it; maybe we can talk after group so that I can give you my full attention").

CONFIDENTIALITY

The group rule of confidentiality may create difficulties in the cases of children who disclose information to the group about sexual, physical, or other forms of severe abuse. On the one hand, you establish the norm of confidentiality because you want the children to feel safe to disclose in the group any family secret they may have. On the other hand, you have the duty to report suspected cases of abuse, and this may be perceived by the child as a violation of the rule of confidentiality and of his or her trust in you and in the group.

This potential problem can be prevented by qualifying the rule of confidentiality in the first group session. The children need to know that you have the obligation to share any information on sexual, physical, or other severe abuse of a child if such information was not disclosed and acted on before. Although this explanation may cause some children to be more inhibited about sharing their personal experiences with the group, it will prevent the betrayal of the child's trust in you and in the group.

SEXUAL HARASSMENT

Younger children may find sexual harassment difficult to understand. However, this issue could be addressed with children if they already have encountered the term in school, in the media, or anywhere else. Sexual harassment can be presented as sexually directed verbal abuse or as a verbal form of sexual abuse aimed at the child's private body parts, sexual behavior, or sexual identity. Children should know that sexual harassment is as wrong as "touch" sexual abuse and should be responded to in the same way.

❏ **Facilitator Notes and Food for Thought**

1. FEELING OF THE DAY (AFRAID)

Fear, the feeling of the day, can be stressful and even paralyzing and thus is often perceived as a negative feeling. However, fear also can be presented to children as an empowering feeling; it tells us that we are at risk and that we need to do something to take care of ourselves. When we are afraid, it is a sign that something is wrong and that we need to ask ourselves what can be done to alleviate the fear. When you discuss with the children times when they felt afraid, also ask them what they did to take care of themselves.

2. "GOOD TOUCH-BAD TOUCH" EXERCISE

Fear often is mixed with feelings of ambiguity and confusion. We are often afraid when we sense that something wrong is happening but cannot identify exactly what is wrong or how to "correct" it. Children, especially in families in which touch was used in both caring and abusive ways, often get confusing messages about the meaning of physical touch and how to respond to it. This confusion may result in either fear of any kind of touch or an inability to trust one's fear as an indicator that something is wrong and that action needs to be taken. The aim of this exercise is to sensitize children to the differences between appropriate and inappropriate touch. Once children are able to make this distinction, they can learn what to do when they are touched inappropriately.

Post on the wall a large drawing of a gender-neutral human figure, front and back. Give children red and green stickers and ask them, in turn, to put the stickers on the figure's body—red ones to mark areas of bad touches and green ones to mark areas of good touches.

Discuss additional possibilities for good and bad touches, the difference between good touch and bad touch (especially when they are in the same area of the body), and the connection between bad touch and different forms of abuse (physical, sexual, and emotional).

3. THE STORY "LITTLE BUNNY LEARNS TO SAY NO"
(Davis & Custer, 1990, reprinted with authors' permission)

Once upon a time there was a soft little bunny who lived with his family in a friendly forest. All day he hopped near his mother and felt very happy. One day his mommy said to him, "I must go to the edge of the forest and see if I can find any clover for our dinner. You stay here and I will be back soon."

Now rabbits love to eat clover, and although the little bunny did not want his mommy to go, he didn't want to be hungry, either, so he said goodbye and watched as his mommy hopped away.

At first the bunny was safe by himself, but, as things would have it, a large mean fox happened by. He told the bunny to do things that the bunny didn't want to do. The little bunny was confused; he had always done what adults told him to do, but now he felt that he shouldn't do what the fox was asking. Then he remembered his mother telling him that he was very smart.

Suddenly he had the answer; he could shout, "No! No! Stop!" in a very loud voice. And the more he shouted, the bigger his voice got. The bunny shouted louder and louder and louder, "No! Stop! I won't do that!" The mean fox tried getting meaner and gruffer to make the bunny do things, but that didn't work. Even though he was very scared, he continued to shout, "No! No!" in a very loud voice.

At last the fox went away. The little bunny was still frightened, but he felt different now. He had discovered that although he was very little compared to the fox, he was powerful in a different way than the fox was. The bunny told his mother all about the fox when she

> **Box 4.19: Basic Instructions for Personal Protection**
> - Say no.
> - Get away, if possible.
> - Tell someone you trust.

returned home. His mommy was very glad that he had told her everything that happened and gave him a big hug. And he smiled as he went to sleep that night because he discovered that a bunny can be smart as a fox.

4. PERSONAL PROTECTION

We recommend that you give the children clear and simple instructions regarding how to protect themselves when someone is trying to harm them. You can write these instructions on a poster or on personal cards. Basic instructions are presented in Box 4.19.

5. PERSONAL SPACE EXERCISE

The aim of this activity is to raise the children's awareness of personal space in general and to sensitize them to their own personal boundaries.

Separate the children into two groups and have them line up facing each other on both sides of the room. Assign a partner from the opposite side of the room to each child. As one of the groups starts advancing toward the other, instruct the members of the stationary group to pay attention to their level of comfort as their designated partner moves toward them and to tell that partner "stop!" when it feels as if the child is getting too close. Repeat the exercise after switching the roles between the two groups.

After the exercise, discuss with the children their personal boundaries, personal levels of comfort, their right to maintain comfortable boundaries around their personal space, occasions when personal boundaries may be violated, and ways of handling these occasions.

Week Eight: Assertiveness

❏ Messages

"I have the right to be safe."
"I can be strong without being abusive."

❏ Desired Outcomes for the Child

1. To be able to identify several personal positive qualities and strengths
2. To know the difference between being strong and being abusive
3. To know that a child has the right to be safe

❏ Outline

Box 4.20: Outline for Session Eight

- Check-in.
- Feeling of the day: strong. [See Facilitator Note 1.]
- Learning the differences between assertiveness, aggressiveness, and passivity. May be done as a group discussion (appropriate posters can be prepared ahead of time) or through a discussion of a story or a film.

Palmer, P. (1977). *The mouse, the monster, and me.* San Luis Obispo, CA: Impact. (Ages 4 to 12)

This book is full of ideas about how young people can grow up to be assertive, make good decisions, and stand up for themselves. The book is interactive, providing activities and questions to help children learn about themselves.

(continued)

Box 4.20: Continued

Mitchell, J. G. (Producer). *Tell 'em how you feel* [Film]. (18 min.). (#4890). Distributed by: MTI Film & Video, 108 Wilmont Rd., Deerfield, IL 60015 (800) 621-2131. (Ages 4 to 9)

It is the story of a child who feels all alone and angry at his parents and best friend. A friendly troll the child meets in the woods teaches him how to handle anger and conflicts without holding in feelings or fighting.

- Assertiveness activity. [See Facilitator Note 2.]
- Safety discussion: What are potentially dangerous situations for the children (including those related to family violence)? Who is responsible for the violence and for stopping it? How can the children protect themselves in dangerous circumstances? [See Facilitator Note 3.]
- Closure: Personal affirmation. "Pass the Squeeze"; Optional message: "I'm a special, lovable person."

❑ General Considerations

ASSERTIVENESS

The aim of this session is to introduce to children the concept of *assertiveness* (as opposed to aggressiveness and passivity) and connect it with their right to be safe. This session is not assertiveness training (a much longer process) and probably will not create noticeable changes in the behavior of most children. It is important to communicate the limitations of this assertiveness session to parents in order to prevent unrealistic expectations.

PREPARING FOR THE END OF GROUP

Children need time to digest the coming end of the group and to prepare for it. Mention to the children in this session that only two more group sessions are left. This may upset some children who enjoyed the group and became attached to group participants and leaders. Children's feelings about the nearing end of the group may be expressed as acting out.

❑ Facilitator Notes and Food for Thought

1. FEELING OF THE DAY (STRONG)

When discussing with the children times when they felt strong, it is important to emphasize at least two ways of being strong: physically and emotionally/mentally ("inside" and "outside" strong). Help the children remember occasions when they felt strong inside and commend them on their strength.

2. ASSERTIVENESS ACTIVITIES

Personal Strengths. Children write (or draw) on a sheet of paper the strengths, good qualities, and things they like about themselves. (This paper may be prepared by the group leaders ahead of time, with a title, decorations, etc.) After the children finish, they hand their papers to the next child in the circle so that each child presents to the group the strengths and qualities of the neighbor.

Developmental differences between younger and older children may be reflected in this exercise. Younger children may find it easier to present their own work to the group. Older children may find it harder to talk about their own qualities if they have internalized social expectations regarding "modesty." Hence, it may be easier for them to have another child present their work.

Cards (based on *In a Pickle: Strategies for Problem Solving,* a game by Janet L. Peal & Carla T. Trade). Group leaders prepare cards, each

Box 4.21: Questions for Assertiveness Exercise

- What should you do if you think your friend has made a bad decision?
- What can you do if your parents make a decision you don't like?
- What can you do if a friend wants you to do her homework for her?
- What can you do if a teacher hugs you in front of the class?
- What can you do when a parent makes you wear clothes you don't like?
- What should you do if a stranger offers you a ride?
- What can you do if you feel sick at school?
- What can you do if you get in trouble for something you didn't do?
- What can you do if you lose your homework on the way to school?
- What can you do if you are at a friend's house and you don't like the food?

referring to a situation that can be dealt with best by an assertive response. The situations should be familiar to the children and can involve group themes.

Sitting in a circle with the cards in a mixed pile in the center, the children, in turn, pick a card and respond to the question on it. After a child answers, other children can give their own solutions. When needed, group leaders can help the children remember a similar situation that happened to them or to someone they know. Examples of questions are presented in Box 4.21.

Puppets. Puppets can be used with or without a puppet theater. A puppet theater can be bought or can be made by spreading a cloth between two chairs. Puppets work best with 4- to 9-year-olds; older children may consider a puppet activity to be too childish.

A. A group leader presents scenes of interactions between two puppets demonstrating passive, aggressive, and assertive behavior. Interactions can be between parent and child, siblings, grandparent and child, children at school, teacher and child,

Box 4.22: A Story on Passive, Aggressive, and Assertive Behaviors

I came to school in the morning and saw Mini sitting on my chair. I was angry at her. I really like my chair, and that's where I can see the chalkboard best. But I decided not to do anything; she probably will move to her own chair later, and then I can go back to my chair.

But she never moved. At the first break, I was already so angry that I went to her and pushed her off the chair. She fell on the floor and got her knees bruised. She cried and told the teacher I hit her, which wasn't true. And then the bell rang and class started again, and she stayed sitting on my chair.

On the second break, I decided to try something else. I went to Mini and asked her why she was sitting on my chair. She said she wanted a change and thought I wouldn't mind. I told her that I do mind and would she please give me my chair back. She said "okay," and though she didn't look too happy about it, she finally gave me back my chair.

child and stranger, and so on. Ideas for scenes can be taken from the questions suggested for the card game. After each scene, the other group leader discusses it with the children: What behavior was demonstrated? How did each puppet feel? How did the children feel watching the interaction? What are the consequences of the demonstrated communication? What are the alternatives to the demonstrated behavior?

B. A group leader manipulates a puppet that tells the children different stories of its life, stories that portray passive, aggressive, and assertive behavior. An example is presented in Box 4.22. The puppet dialogues with the children about each interaction, using the topics for discussion mentioned in (A) above.

C. The group leader's puppet displays aggressive communication or behavior toward a puppet held by a child. Using a puppet, each child demonstrates a response of assertive communication. Each child should have a chance to do this in turn.

Examples of aggressive communications are name calling, teasing, threatening, and demanding something the child has and does not want to give up. The group leader must be careful not to hurt the child while acting aggressively.

Instruct each child to stick up for him- or herself in an assertive manner. (The child can be coached by the other group leader or by the other children.) Scenes may include disrespectful or nonresponsive reactions to the child's assertive responses. However, it is important to end each scene with the group leader's puppet showing respect for the child's assertiveness. After the scene is over, group leaders can discuss with the child how it felt when the puppet was aggressive and when the child responded assertively. An example of a possible scene is presented in Box 4.23.

Role Play. The boundaries can be very thin between real life and simulation of real life through role play. Role playing can evoke intense emotions in the children; be prepared to deal with these emotions and be careful not to push children beyond what they are capable of doing.

A. Taking turns, each child role-plays with a group leader, who communicates aggressively with the child. The other group leader acts as the child's coach or "alter ego," encouraging him or her to try different communication styles in response to the aggressive behavior. Ultimately, this exercise should demonstrate that the most effective way of dealing with aggressive communication is by responding assertively. After the role play is completed, group leaders facilitate a discussion with the child about his or her feelings and thoughts during the exercise.

Box 4.23: An Example of Assertiveness Coaching

Puppet Look at your shirt! Who heard of a boy wearing a black shirt!?

Child Your shirt is not much better! It's ugly!

Puppet Yeah?! Your shirt is uglier!

Coach What do you think will happen next?

Child I don't know. We'll probably fight.

Coach It seems like you're already fighting. Is there another way of answering him that wouldn't lead to a fight?

Child Maybe I can just leave and not talk with him.

Coach Yes, that's one good idea. But what if you want to stay here?

Child Maybe I can tell him I don't care what he thinks about my shirt.

Coach And that you like it. Try telling him that.

Child I don't care what you think about my shirt! I like it and that's all that counts. Now please leave me alone.

Puppet You're smart. You know how not to get into a fight for some stupid teasing.

B. Various situations are written on index cards that portray passive, aggressive, and assertive communication. Roles are specified for a protagonist and other actors. Each child, in turn, picks a card, reads it to the group, and assigns other children to other roles. Group leaders can act as coaches or "alter egos" for the acting children. The situation is acted out and then discussed with the facilitation of the group leaders. The discussion should explore thoughts, feelings, possible motives, and alternative behaviors. (Ages 10 to 12)

C. Group leaders act out different scenes demonstrating passive, aggressive, assertive, and passive-aggressive behaviors. Children are asked ahead of time to pay close attention to how and what each actor is saying. Each scene then is discussed with the children, with an emphasis on the behavior, its label, and associated feelings (e.g., "How do you think the bully felt?").

3. RESPONSIBILITY FOR THE CHILD'S SAFETY

We hold the parents and other adults in the child's life to be responsible for the child's safety and well-being. However, under circumstances of family violence and other dangerous situations in which a child's safety is at risk, we want the children to know they need to take care of themselves. Children's ability, right, and responsibility to protect themselves do not replace the parents' responsibility for the child's safety, but rather are a way of empowering children who find themselves in dangerous situations.

Week Nine: Protection Planning

❏ **Message**

"I have the right to be safe."

❏ **Desired Outcomes for the Child**

1. To identify places to go and people to call in dangerous situations and cases of emergency
2. To learn how to use the telephone and what to say when calling police or another helper
3. To know that group ends the next week

❏ **Outline**

Box 4.24: Outline for Session Nine

- Check-in. [See Facilitator Note 1.]
- Feeling of the day: happy. [See Facilitator Note 2.]
- Review the "safety discussion" from the previous week. [See Facilitator Note 3.]
- Work individually on Personal Protection Planning (PPP). [See Facilitator Note 4]: Talk with each child about whom to call and where to go in dangerous situations or in cases of emergency. Write this information on a personal card (older children can write their own personal cards). [See Facilitator Note 5.]
- Practice calling the police or another helper on the telephone. The call first is modeled by a group leader and then is practiced by each child. [See Facilitator Note 6.]
- Draw a picture on the back of the PPP card. Optional topics: "Abuse is not okay," "I deserve to be safe."
- Briefly discuss the coming end of the group. Make a group decision about what kind of snack to have for the last day. [See Facilitator Note 7.]
- Closure: Personal affirmation. "Pass the Squeeze"; Optional message: "I have the right to be safe."

❏ **Facilitator Notes and Food for Thought**

1. CHECK-IN

The check-in may be an opportunity for group leaders and children to express their feelings about the coming end of the group. You may want to ask the children directly how they feel about it or model for them by expressing your feelings about separating from them and from the group. Allow the children to express a range of feelings, including relief, about the ending of the group.

2. FEELING OF THE DAY (HAPPY)

We chose "happy" for this session because it is the next-to-the-last session and we like to end the group with a positive feeling. Although some children will be sad that the group is ending, it is our experience that at least some of them will be happy and relieved.

3. SAFETY DISCUSSION

Talk with the children about the circumstances under which they should call 911 or others for help. (Not every community has a 911 system. If your group is in a community that does not have a 911 system, teach the children the seven-digit phone number of the local police.) We are concerned that children may think it is their responsibility to "save" their mothers and stop violent events by calling 911. Such messages are reinforced by some films (e.g., *It's Not Always Happy at My House* and *The Crown Prince*) and can add to children's feelings of guilt for failing to prevent or stop the violence. For this reason, it is important that the discussion emphasize the children's right and responsibility to protect *themselves*, rather than others.

Remind the children that the perpetrator is responsible for the violence and that the adults are responsible for stopping it. At the same time, let the children know that at times they may need to protect themselves from being physically hurt and then they can call 911. They also may choose to call 911 when they see that someone else is in danger, but it is not their responsibility to do so.

Talk about these self-protection issues with the children's parents in the parenting group or individually. Recommend that parents talk and decide with their children under what circumstances the child should call 911.

4. PERSONAL PROTECTION PLANNING (PPP)

Children need to be able to protect themselves from risk both inside and outside their homes. The aim of a personal protection plan (PPP) is to equip the children with some practical, realistic, and usable skills to be used in cases of emergency. This session does not focus on the psychological aspects of these circumstances; however, some discussion of potential risks in the child's life may be required if the child denies the possibility of future family violence and refuses to do protection planning. Although there is no need to force the possibility of future violence into the child's consciousness, it can be pointed out as a realistic possibility that requires some consideration.

Each child needs to identify safe places to go or to hide in when he or she feels threatened or senses danger. Inside the home, these places could be the child's room, a sibling's room, and the basement. Safe places outside the home could be the homes of neighbors, friends, or relatives. Help the child think of possible safe places by discussing actual times when he or she felt the need for a safe place. Check with the child to ensure that each suggested place is truly safe and that it is a realistic option.

All children should know how to call the police in case of emergency; in most cases, this number is 911, but many rural areas are not connected to a 911 network yet, so the seven-digit phone number of the police department must be called. If possible, each child should have access to phone numbers of trusted relatives, friends, or neighbors who live nearby.

5. PERSONAL PROTECTION PLANNING CARD

The PPP card gives the child quick access to critical information in times of emergency. Use 5 × 7 index cards (see Figure 4.3). One side of the card is personalized and decorated with the child's own drawing of a theme, such as "Abuse is not okay" or "I have the right to be safe." The other side contains the child's first name, the child's self-portrait, and PPP information, consisting of a list of safe places and phone numbers that can be used in cases of emergency. If needed, this list can be qualified by time of day, type of event, or other restrictions. Write the PPP information on the cards for younger children and supervise the older children who can write it themselves.

After the work on the card is completed, laminate it. Lamination can be done after this session and the card given to the children during the last session. Lamination is significant because it protects the card and makes it look "official" and "real." You may want to tape a quarter onto each card in case the children will need to use a pay phone to call for help.

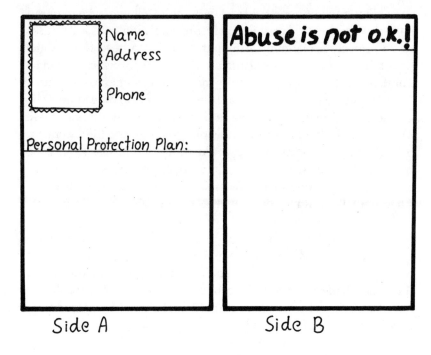

Figure 4.3. Personal Protection Planning Card

6. PRACTICE PHONE CALLS

The purpose of this activity is to give the children an opportunity to practice calling the police and to coach them to do it effectively. Depending on the children's ages, either a toy or a real (disconnected) phone can be used. Start by modeling a 911 (or seven-digit police number) call and then coach each of the children in turn. Emphasize the elements listed in Box 4.25.

This activity may evoke strong feelings in the children, especially for those who have had a previous experience with calling the police or with having the police come to their homes. Remind the children that this is only an exercise and help the ones who experience triggered emotions.

Box 4.25: Instructions for Calling 911/Police

- The child must speak clearly and loudly (if it is safe to do so).
- The call should be concise but also include the reason for calling and the child's name, address, and phone number. (In some areas, the caller's number appears automatically on the 911 operator's screen.)
- The children should say "Please come quickly!" and, if they have the time, ask whether more information is needed at the end of the call.

---

7. PREPARATION FOR LAST SESSION

The last group session is an occasion for both the sadness of separation and feelings of relief and accomplishment after the hard work done in previous weeks. Acknowledge both.

As part of celebrating the end of the group, you can let the children have a snack of their choice. You also may give them a little souvenir, an "I am special" badge, and a "diploma" or a "certificate of completion," all of which require advance preparation. (For details, see the "Facilitator Notes and Food for Thought" section for Week Ten.)

Week Ten: Review and Good-Bye

❏ **Messages**

"It's sad to say good-bye."
"You were great! You deserve the best!"

❏ **Desired Outcomes for the Child**

1. To realize that this is the end of the group and to express some related emotions

2. To acknowledge his or her accomplishments and to feel proud of him- or herself [See Facilitator Note 1.]

❑ **Outline**

Box 4.26: Outline for Session Ten

- Check-in. Include how the children feel about the fact that this is the last group session.
- Discussion: "How did you feel when you first came to the group? Have these feelings changed over time?" Facilitate the discussion by having the children act out how they felt entering the group room on the first day and how they felt entering the room today.
- Review and evaluate the group in an open group discussion: What did the children learn in the group? What did they like and not like about it? What were their favorite things in the group? What would they have done differently? [See Facilitator Note 2.]
- *Ages 4 to 9.* Story: "The Children's Star." Give the children a "star" souvenir at the end of the story. [See Facilitator Note 3.]
- *Ages 7 to 12.* A souvenir T-shirt: Give each child a plain T-shirt and some fabric crayons, markers, or paint. Ask the children to write their names or short messages on each other's T-shirts.
- Give the children a Certificate of Completion. [See Facilitator Note 4.]
- Positive affirmation [See Facilitator Note 5.]: Say something positive to each of the children that can be related to the work they have done in the group. Then pin on each child's shirt an "I am special!" badge. [See Facilitator Note 6.]
- "Pass the Squeeze" game. If possible, each child passes his or her own message around the circle. [See Facilitator Note 7.] Optional messages: "It's sad to say good-bye." "I'll miss you, but I'll remember you and what we did together." "Good-bye! We were great! We deserve the best!"

❏ **General Considerations**

SCHEDULING A FAMILY SESSION

A family session follows the end of the group. It includes the group leaders, the child, and the parents. If the parents are in the parenting group, the family session can be scheduled with the help of the parenting group leader. Sometime during the last group session, let the children know about the upcoming family session and its purpose. This will help them prepare to come to the agency one more time to talk about the group.

❏ **Facilitator Notes and Food for Thought**

1. THE CHILDREN'S ACCOMPLISHMENTS IN THE GROUP

Many of the children's accomplishments are intangible. Furthermore, each child, depending on individual characteristics and history, will have a different list of accomplishments. The children may need your help in identifying their achievements in the group. Commend the children for being brave enough to participate in the group and to deal with painful issues, for being good listeners and friends to other group members, for learning new ideas, and for expressing uncomfortable thoughts and feelings.

2. REVIEW AND EVALUATION OF THE GROUP

The purpose of this activity is to allow the children to express their opinions and feelings about the group and to give group leaders a sense of what the children learned in the group. This is not a formal evaluation of the program; rather, it is an opportunity to empower the children by giving them the message that their opinions and ideas are valid, important, and useful. With older children, you may want to do part of the evaluation in writing to allow children to give anonymous feedback.

3. THE STORY "THE CHILDREN'S STAR" (original idea by Jim Brink)

Once upon a time in a faraway and mountainous country lived many children. Each child lived in a house with his or her family. Because the land was so very steep, it was dangerous for the children to wander or play too far from their homes. For children who had brothers or sisters, it wasn't so bad. But even so, none of the children ever had a chance to play with children in other houses in this mountainous area. It was very lonely, and sometimes the children didn't get along with their brothers or sisters so they got into fights. Many of these children also had moms and dads who would get angry with each other. Some children even saw their mom being hit by her partner or by their other parent. It was scary and sad.

One night a beautiful colored light appeared in the windows of all the houses of all the families in the mountains. The children were awakened by this wonderful light. They got out of bed and were very surprised to find that none of their moms and dads were awakened by this light. So the children went outside to see the beautiful light. It was so strong that some children could see other houses and even some of the other children. Forgetting that it was night and how they all had been told never to wander away, the children started walking toward the light.

Now the shimmering light was really a star that had come very close to the mountains, over a valley. Children came from all over the mountains to the valley, drawn and guided by the light. They all played and danced and sang. Each one felt very happy and safe and, most important, not alone. Then, as day began to dawn, the children started back for home. As they were leaving, the star burst into a thousand million little pieces. Each of the children took a piece of the star as they headed home in the early light of dawn.

Each child quietly went back to bed. Some of the children woke up in the morning and thought they had dreamed about playing with the other children under the beautiful light of the star. But then, they all found the pieces of the star they had taken with them and knew that this wasn't a dream and that they weren't alone anymore. And every time they looked at the star pieces, they remembered being together with the other children and how happy that was.

Figure 4.4.

4. CERTIFICATE OF COMPLETION (COC)

Multipurpose program certificates of completion (COCs) can be bought in paper-products stores. You also could make a unique COC for your group, either on a computer or by hand (see Figure 4.4 for an example). Each COC should include the program's name, the child's name, the date, and the signatures of the group leaders. Another option is to include the number of sessions the child participated in. This can be especially useful if a child has missed many sessions and needs to go through the group again. It is our experience that older children like formal-looking COCs, while younger children relate better to decorative and colorful COCs.

5. POSITIVE AFFIRMATION

After affirming themselves in previous group sessions, in the last session the children can give positive affirmations to each other. Being explicitly valued by their friends is a powerful contribution to children's self-esteem. Use this option with older children and only in groups in which there is minimal risk of the children not finding anything positive to say about their friends.

It is usually safer to ask each child to say "something good" about one other child—for example, the next child in the circle. Tactfully help a child who cannot find any positive affirmation to say regarding the other child's good qualities or talents. Never leave a child unaffirmed. Box 4.27 contains an example.

6. "I AM SPECIAL!" BADGE

Ask the children to close their eyes when you pin the badges on their shirts. This surprise effect is especially strong with younger children. The badge can be made in several ways. We use shiny golden cardboard stars sold as Christmas decorations, attach a safety pin to the back of the star, and write "I am special!" on the front.

7. "PASS THE SQUEEZE"

You may need to help the children put together their messages. Tactfully censor messages that conflict with the spirit of the group. For example, we asked a 10-year-old boy who suggested the message "We hate the girls!" to find another, more positive and inclusive one.

Box 4.27: An Example of Positive Affirmation Exercise

Group Leader Rachel, what good things can you say about Sharon?

Rachel I like her shoes.

Group Leader Yes, Sharon's shoes are very nice. Can you think about other things, things she is good at, nice qualities she has?

Rachel Well, I don't really know things like that about her. We only know each other here.

Group Leader That's right, but here in the group we got to know several good things about Sharon. It's enough to look at the walls . . .

Mike She's good at painting!

Rachel Oh, yeah! She is a real good artist, the way she draws all these animals.

Group Leader Now, can you say that to Sharon?

Rachel (turns to Sharon) You are a very good artist. Maybe the second best in the group.

Family Session

❑ **Main Theme**

Review the group and its influence on the child and make recommendations for future services.

❑ **Desired Outcomes for the Parents and the Child**

1. To discuss together group content and activities

2. To feel that they have had the opportunity to give their feedback on the group and that their feedback was heard by the group leaders

3. To have a clear idea about the child's therapeutic needs and to learn about available and appropriate services

❏ Outline

Box 4.28: Outline for Family Session

- Briefly review the group content [see Facilitator Note 1]. This may be done together with the child [see Facilitator Note 2].
- The child gives feedback on the group: What did the child like and not like about the group? What were especially enjoyable, difficult, or meaningful moments during the group? What things would the child have done differently or would have liked to add? What did the child gain from the group (if at all)?
- The parent gives feedback regarding the group's influence on the child: Did the parent notice any changes in the child's attitudes, expression of feelings, or behavior during the time of the group? What were they? Did the parent talk with the child about these changes? What does the parent think the child gained from the group (if at all)?
- Discuss the child's therapeutic needs [see Facilitator Note 3] and available services within the agency or outside the agency [see Facilitator Note 4].

❏ General Considerations

SESSION PARTICIPANTS

If possible, both group leaders should participate in the family session. Each of you can make a unique contribution to the session with your individual perspective on the group and your relationship with the child. Prepare for the family session ahead of time; plan what you would like to say to the parents and the child and who of

Box 4.29: Potential Sources of Stress in Family Session

- The child may not wish to reopen and discuss issues related to family violence that he or she boxed up after the group ended. Such a discussion may be even more threatening and uncomfortable for the child in the presence of the parents.
- The child may feel uncomfortable being the focus of the session. In this respect, the family session may be associated with school conferences in which the child's performance is evaluated and criticized.
- Some children may fear that their parents will disclose "family secrets" to the group leaders, thus damaging the image the children created during the group.

the group leaders will do what. Be prepared for the possibility that new information will be provided by the family in the session. Such information may require you to rethink your recommendations.

In thinking about parent participation, consider issues of efficiency and safety for both the child and the abused parent. Parents who participated in the parenting group and who maintained communication with the group leaders throughout the group usually are the ones who take part in the family session. A parent who was not involved with the child's group prior to the family session or who is currently abusive should not be part of the family session. When you are in doubt about the safety of either the parent or the child, discretely consult the nonabusive parent regarding the participation of the other parent. The family session may need to be extended when two or more siblings participated in groups at the same time.

CHILD'S STRESS RELATED TO THE FAMILY SESSION

Our study found the family session to be potentially stressful for the child for the reasons listed in Box 4.29. Much of this stress can be reduced by informing the child about the family session ahead of time (in the last group session) and by explaining the purpose and expected structure. It is especially important to stress to the child that the purpose of the session is not to evaluate him or her, but rather to hear from the child and his or her parents what they think about the group. Furthermore, we found that children who had a positive group experience or good relationships with the group leaders were happy to visit the agency and the group leaders again.

MAINTAINING THE SESSION'S FOCUS ON THE CHILD

Some parents may take the opportunity provided in the family session to talk about their own concerns, needs, and problems. Focus on the parent's concerns regarding the child and on family issues. Prevent the session from turning into an individual or couple counseling session.

❑ Facilitator Notes and Food for Thought

1. GROUP REVIEW

The purpose of the group review is to facilitate open communication about the group between the child and his or her parents by talking about it in the presence of all of them. We would like the child and the parents to know that "the other knows" and to prevent the group's content from becoming a secret the child holds from the parents.

When reviewing the group, remember the rule of confidentiality and do not share with the parents specific things that were said or done by the child; rather, describe in general what was learned and done in the group and what was achieved by the child. Review your case notes (or the Desired Outcomes Evaluation Forms [from Appendix B]) before the family session to refresh your memory about the child's achievements in the group.

2. CHILD'S PARTICIPATION IN REVIEWING THE GROUP

Be careful not to turn the group review into a stressful test situation for the child. Do not start the review by asking the child, "What do you remember from the group?" or "What did you learn in the group?" Rather, start the review yourself and invite the child to join you. Group review with the child can be facilitated by having in the room some of the props and posters used in the group sessions.

3. DISCUSSION OF THE CHILD'S NEEDS

You may wish to conduct this part of the session with only the parents. In this case, ask the child to play in another room that was prepared ahead of time. This would be especially important if the child has a special problem that he or she is not fully aware of or if you suspect the child's presence blocks the parents from talking about certain issues. If it is not possible to have the child play in another room, be mindful about the way you convey your assessment and recommendations so as not to shame or embarrass the child.

4. ALTERNATIVES FOR FUTURE INTERVENTION

One of the important objectives of the family session is to discuss with the parents the child's need for additional intervention and, if necessary, to make appropriate referrals. Some of the children will need no additional professional intervention. For those who do, you may want to suggest one or more of the options presented in Box 4.30.

These services can be provided through your agency or by outside referral, depending on the agency's resources. If appropriate, continued intervention with the family in the agency is recommended because trust and familiarity have been established already with the agency and its staff.

Box 4.30: Alternatives for Future Intervention

- Repeating the group immediately or at a later time (for children who missed a critical number of group sessions or who could benefit significantly from repeating the group)
- Individual therapy around issues of family violence (when the child's needs could not be met in a group setting or require more intensive therapy)
- Further physical or psychological diagnosis (when available information does not allow an accurate assessment)
- Specialized intervention around such issues as child abuse (physical, sexual, ritualistic, emotional), learning difficulties, and behavioral problems
- Family therapy
- Intervention with parents (e.g., through a parenting group, Parents Anonymous, parent individual or group therapy)

5

Parenting Group

The 10-week parenting group described here may be offered as a voluntary option for parents whose children participate in a children's group. The approach used in the parenting group is psychoeducational. The first half of each of the first nine sessions consists of an educational activity around the day's topic. In the second half, parents are given the opportunity to support each other by sharing child-related needs and concerns. The concluding session is devoted to unfinished business from the previous nine sessions, to summary, and to evaluation and feedback.

In addition to its psychoeducational focus, the parenting group provides a convenient and safe setting for keeping parents informed about the weekly content of the children's groups and for discussing questions and concerns they may have regarding their child's group experience.

In this chapter, we briefly describe nine major educational topics for the first nine sessions of the parenting group. The discussion of

AUTHORS' NOTE: We thank Joan Bilinkoff for her contribution to this chapter.

each topic includes two sections: "Rationale" for including the topic in the parenting group and "Facilitator Notes and Food for Thought." Unlike the previous chapter, this one is not a step-by-step guide for conducting a parenting group; rather, it aims at providing you with a basic idea of the content and structure of such a group. You will need to add supplementary material in order to conduct a parenting group. For detailed curricula of parenting groups in the context of domestic violence, we suggest you examine manuals by Pence, Hardesty, Steil, Soderberg, and Ottman (1991), Mathews, Matter, and Montgomery (1990), and chapters by Bilinkoff (1995) and Mathews (1995).

The purpose of the first four topics covered in this chapter ("The Effects on Children of Witnessing Violence," "The Effects of Early Life Experiences on Parenting," "Child Development," and "Parents' Rights/Children's Rights") is to provide information; to challenge attitudes, values, beliefs, and assumptions; and to create new insight. The subsequent five topics ("Discipline Versus Punishment," "Self-Esteem in Children," "Communication," "Sibling Relationships," "Changing Families") focus on skill development. Learning new skills prior to changing dysfunctional or erroneous attitudes and beliefs may lead to a misuse of power and control. We recommend, therefore, addressing the topics in the order they are presented.

Introduction: General Considerations

We recommend that children's and parent's groups meet concurrently, in separate rooms. As we stated earlier, through the parenting group the parents are informed of the weekly content of the childrens groups and can discuss questions and concerns they may have regarding their child's group experience. It is important to inform parents about the content of children's group sessions for several reasons. First, sharing this information with the parents prevents it from becoming a secret between child and parent, thus permitting the children to share thoughts and feelings about the group experience with their parents. This, in turn, may lessen the child's feelings of shame, guilt, loneliness, and isolation.

Second, prior knowledge of the group content can help parents anticipate, accept, and be prepared for their child's emotional and behavioral reaction to the group. Third, parents can reinforce messages and behaviors learned in the children's group, thus assisting in integrating group content into their child's everyday life.

The information suggested here is based on work with mothers—victims/survivors of woman battering. We believe, however, that parenting groups should be offered separately for both parents—victims/survivors and abusers. Both mothers and fathers will benefit from discussing parenting issues, learning parenting skills, and being involved in their children's group experience. Although we encourage work with abusers on parenting issues, the special issues involved in such work are beyond the scope of our current experience.

We recommend not including abusers in groups with victims/survivors. It is our experience that even when the participating abusers have completed a structured domestic abuse program and have stopped using abusive behavior toward their partners and children, and even when all group members agreed to include them in the group, their presence intimidates and blocks participation by some victims/survivors, and power and control issues often are raised.

Ideally, victims/survivors will have completed their own domestic violence program before enrolling their children in groups and participating in the parenting group. We have found that completers are better able to stay focused on their children's needs, rather than focus on their own survival.

We recommend that the parenting support group be cofacilitated (female-male team when parents are heterosexual, same sex when parents are gay or lesbian). This arrangement provides an opportunity to model a healthy working relationship, including healthy communication, flexibility in role division, and mutual respect for each other's thoughts, opinions, and feelings. This model requires that facilitators communicate and coordinate planning in advance of the session.

Facilitators need to be clear and in agreement about their long- and short-term goals and objectives. Keep in mind that each group is different and that objectives may need to be revised. Other areas to consider are philosophical assumptions, styles of teaching/therapy, who takes the lead and when, and how to resolve differences in opinion.

Cultural and ethnic differences often affect parenting. Be aware of your own biases and be knowledgeable of the different values and belief systems held by different ethnic groups represented. For example, a lesbian mother may encounter homophobic attitudes from other participants regarding her parenting, or a Native American parent may need support in discussing the influence of government boarding schools' experience on her parenting. Seek supervision if necessary to clarify these issues. Also do not assume that all mothers are custodial parents and that all parents are in a heterosexual relationship. Be aware of and work on your own biases and avoid using sexist language.

At the first session, address confidentiality and the limits of confidentiality (see discussion in Chapter 2) and establish expectations and rules regarding group structure, content, attendance, and punctuality.

Help solve individual problems that parents bring to the group, but at the same time keep a "group focus" rather than an individual one. While talking about individual issues, repeatedly include other group members for questions, ideas, and feedback. Attempt to teach group members concepts that can be generalized to other situations and areas.

Be aware that participants may have other agendas (e.g., trying to make sense of their victimization, venting anger at their abuser, getting support for difficulties at work). Attempt, however, to keep the group focused on the children and on parenting and refer parents to individual or couple therapy if appropriate. Be a model for parents in the group by demonstrating positive, constructive feedback—catch parents doing something well—and acknowledge and affirm positive changes that parents are making.

Leading a parenting group may bring up strong feelings about your own experiences with parenting, as a child or as a parent. You may discover also that you have some strong opinions about "right" and "wrong" parenting. Support yourself by discussing these issues with a supervisor or colleagues.

The Effects on Children of Witnessing Violence

❏ **Rationale**

Violence is a learned behavior. Many abusers and some victims/ survivors have a family history of abuse as victims and/or as witnesses. Children who witness violence are at increased risk for developing emotional and behavioral problems (see Chapter 1). These children, their parents, and society at large cannot afford to turn their backs

Violence is a learned behavior.

and deny that these problems exist (Jaffe et al., 1990).

It is our experience that some parents are not aware of how their children have been affected by witnessing violence at home. Defining domestic violence and awareness of the effects of violence on children provide parents with a context for understanding their children's behavior. Consequently, parents are placed in a better position to help their children with witnessing-related problematic behavior. Acquiring information and the development of empathy regarding the effects of witnessing violence can have a positive impact on parents' approach to discipline.

❏ **Facilitator Notes and Food for Thought**

The effects of witnessing violence on children are physical, emotional, social, cognitive, and behavioral. Cover all of these areas with the parents (see Jaffe et al., 1990; Pence et al., 1991). Instruct parents not to generalize all of these effects to their own children; rather, encourage parents to look for the individual ways in which their children were affected by the violence.

An awareness of the effects of witnessing violence may elicit in parents strong feelings of guilt and shame about being "bad" parents. Help parents use this potentially painful learning process as an opportunity to view their children from a different perspective, as well as discover new ways of disciplining and relating to their children.

Holding on to shame and guilt may prevent parents from making necessary changes in their relationships with their children. Reinforce parents' self-esteem; affirm parents for all of the work they have done to get themselves and their children to groups and note that facing oneself and making changes takes a great deal of courage.

The films *It's Not Always Happy at My House, Secret Wounds, Enfantillage,* and *The Crown Prince* (see Chapter 4, Weeks Four and Five) can be used to facilitate parents' understanding of the effects of violence on children. Suggest that parents discuss the films with their children after viewing them.

The Effects of Early Life Experiences on Parenting

❑ **Rationale**

Early life experiences that shape our development throughout childhood continue to influence us as adult parents. An awareness of these powerful influences allows parents to make conscious choices about aspects of their family of origin that they wish to include or to exclude in their current families. Parents do not need to be victims of their past by repeating the same mistakes their own parents made.

❑ **Facilitator Notes and Food for Thought**

You may want to provide parents with a list of areas of early life experiences and discuss with them how one or more of these areas currently affect their parenting. Parents can examine which of these influences they want to hold on to and which they wish to replace. Areas of early life experiences to be addressed can include, but are not limited to, those listed in Box 5.1.

Box 5.1: Areas of Early Life Experiences

- Relationships with parents and siblings
- View of parents' relationship
- Family communication and conflict resolution patterns
- Moving
- Family social life
- Financial circumstances and norms
- Chemical abuse
- Discipline
- Sexuality
- Boundaries
- Family rituals
- Separation
- Divorce and remarriage
- Family best and worst times
- Vacations
- Peer relationships
- Friendships
- Make-believe friends
- School
- Significant and nurturing adult figures

The group is an opportunity for parents to gain insight on these issues. Keep a group focus by encouraging participants to give feedback and support to one another. Avoid carrying out extensive individual counseling in group or focusing only on a few participants to the exclusion of others.

State up-front that exploring family-of-origin issues can elicit strong, unresolved feelings. Encourage parents to be cognizant of the intensity of their feelings, which can be an indication of unresolved issues. Be attuned to, acknowledge, and affirm indications of new insights and behavioral changes in parents.

Note that parents are not the only influences in their children's lives. Hence they deserve neither all the blame nor all the credit for their children's course of development. Encourage parents to continue to reflect on their early life experiences and their impact on parenting in the weeks to come. Assignments can be given to facilitate this process; keeping a journal of one's reactions to group content is strongly recommended to parents.

Child Development

❏ **Rationale**

Children who have been traumatized by witnessing violence in their families may not progress smoothly through the developmental stages. Jaffe and his colleagues (Jaffe et al., 1990) suggest that "the emotional development of children is intimately connected with the safety and nurturance provided by their environment" (p. 34). Knowledge of child development will help parents of child witnesses of violence identify and respond to developmental problems in their children.

In general, parents' knowledge of developmental stages and their associated tasks (a) increases the probability that children's changing developmental needs will be satisfied, (b) helps parents maintain realistic expectations regarding their child's development and understand "misbehavior" that is actually developmentally appropriate behavior, and (c) creates a long-term context for parenting and helps them observe and appreciate their child's achievement of developmental tasks.

❏ **Facilitator Notes and Food for Thought**

Although the children of this parenting group's members are between the ages of 4 and 12, it is advisable to discuss developmental stages through adolescence. This will allow parents to anticipate the upcoming needs of their children. Some parents already may have children in their teens, and it may be necessary to schedule two group sessions to cover all of this material.

Inform parents that age-specific developmental tasks are not absolute. Children begin developmental stages at different times and continue to refine developmental tasks in later stages. Include in the discussion of developmental tasks ways in which parents can foster or hinder development (see Mathews et al., 1990; Pence et al., 1991). Connect the effects of witnessing violence with specific developmental stages (see Jaffe et al., 1990).

An awareness of children's changing needs may evoke guilt in some participants for not being "good enough" parents. Rather than focus on guilt, encourage parents to look at how they can help their children grow up to be healthy and competent adults. Help parents recognize their positive responses to their children and how they can expand and reframe those responses.

Parents' Rights/Children's Rights

❑ Rationale

Our patriarchal culture emphasizes the duties of women and children toward society in general and men in particular. Women are expected to be in charge of the nurturing and caretaking tasks of the family, such as cooking, cleaning, managing the home, being in charge of family rituals, and doing the majority of child care. Men are expected to be in charge of the executive and managerial functions of the family, such as earning money and making family financial decisions. Although some consciousness-raising has been achieved by the women's liberation movement, the men's rights movement, and the children's rights movement, most women and men are still rigidly confined to traditional gender roles. The adherence to these roles prevents both genders from having mutually nurturing, honest, and respectful relationships with each other.

The notion of "parents' rights" challenges the culturally sanctioned role of the selfless, self-scarifying, ever-patient, ever-perfect parent and substitutes it with a more reasonable human role. It empowers parents by encouraging them to meet their needs within other significant roles in their lives. The notion of "children's rights" challenges another cultural belief that our children are our property and generally have no rights.

❏ **Facilitator Notes and Food for Thought**

Provide parents with a list of parents' rights and children's rights as a basis for discussion. Box 5.2 contains an example of such a list.

Encourage parents to talk about their feelings related to parents' and children's rights. Family-of-origin experiences can shed light on the source of some of these feelings. Help parents develop a sense of

---

Box 5.2a: Parents' Rights

- You have a right not to be perfect.
- You have a right to put yourself first sometimes.
- You have a right to your own opinions and convictions.
- You have a right to be your own final judge.
- You have a right to your feelings and to express them appropriately.
- You have a right to change your mind.
- You have a right to choose not to respond to a situation.
- You have a right to say no.
- You have a right to set boundaries.
- You have a right to ask for what you want or need.
- You have a right to ask for help or emotional support.
- You have a right to take time for yourself.
- You have a right to have a social/romantic/sexual life.
- You have a right to have private time with your partner.
- You have a right to pursue your own interests/career.
- You have a right to be happy.

Domestic Abuse Project, 1993.

Box 5.2b: Children's Rights

- Children have a right to be children.
- Children have a right to have fun.
- Children have a right to have feelings and ideas and to express them.
- Children have a right to ask for what they need.
- Children have a right to some secrets.
- Children have a right to say no.
- Children have a right to privacy.
- Children have a right to make certain choices.
- Children have a right to be respected.
- Children have a right to be accepted for who they are.
- Children have a right to be nurtured and cared for.
- Children have a right to a support system, including peers and supportive adults.
- Children have a right to know their limits.
- Children have a right to rewards and natural consequences.
- Children have a right to be protected from abuse and neglect.
- Children have a right to be believed.
- Children have a right to a relationship with their parents.
- Children have a right to be protected from knowledge beyond their years.
- Children have a right not to worry about grown-ups' problems.
- Children have a right to be happy.

Children's Rights from Mathews, D., Matter, L., & Montgomery, M. (1990). *Wilder Parenting Manual*. Amherst H. Wilder Foundation, Community Assistance Program, 650 Marshall Ave., St. Paul, MN 55104, (612) 221-0048. Published by KidsRights, and reprinted with permission.

assertiveness about their own needs and encourage them to take care of themselves. Suggest that parents view themselves as a model for their children in the areas of self-care and self-respect.

Children's rights may be perceived by some parents as threatening, particularly if the parents feel vulnerable or powerless at the time. Remind parents that they have a responsibility to meet the needs of their children and that one of the best ways to ensure that this occurs is to make certain their own needs are also met.

Acknowledge that there is continuing tension in the balance of self-care with care of children. A discussion of the concepts of *respect* and *equality* can facilitate a better understanding of parents' and children's rights; for example, What is the relationship between self-respect and mutual respect, and how are these played throughout parents' lives? Are children equal to adults? Do children have the same rights as adults?

Discipline Versus Punishment

❑ **Rationale**

Our culture has a long history of seeing children as property and their behavior as a mirror reflection of our failures and successes as parents. Until very recently, physical punishment was sanctioned by our culture as a way of maintaining control and enforcing unquestioning obedience from our children (Pleck, 1987).

Current child-rearing experts now emphasize "discipline" instead of "punishment." Punishment, on the one hand, is viewed as generally unrelated to misbehavior, offering few options and solutions and demanding unrealistic expectations from the child. Punishment discourages children from taking responsibility for their own behavior. Finally, it creates fear, intimidation, and a very dangerous assumption for child witnesses: "People who love me, hurt me."

Discipline, on the other hand, can require children to take responsibility for their behavior and teach self-control and problem solving. It may facilitate development of a positive self-esteem and inner sense of power and teaches children that people who love you can treat you respectfully even when they are angry with you (Dinkmeyer & McKay, 1989; Pence et al., 1991).

❑ Facilitator Notes and Food for Thought

Provide parents with definitions of discipline and punishment and discuss the differences between them. Some parents may be confused about the difference between the two; be prepared to give examples to clarify these concepts.

Remind parents that discipline is taking place in the context of an overall parent-child relationship. Encourage parents to develop a positive relationship with their child through a variety of shared activities. Within a positive relationship, children may be more receptive to the lessons they learn through being disciplined.

Like discussion of other topics mentioned earlier, the discussion of this topic may elicit a defensive response in parents because of mistakes they have made in the past and a sense of inadequacy as a parent. Help parents look at mistakes they have made as a learning opportunity. Recognition of these mistakes is a necessary step for change. Remind parents that they are a model for their children and that children learn from the ways parents deal with their own mistakes. Encourage parents to apologize to their child when they have made a mistake.

Discuss logical and natural consequences as two forms of discipline. Encourage parents to allow their child to fail and learn through natural and logical consequences. Also encourage them to be mindful of their child's developmental stage so that they have realistic expectations, as well as use stage-appropriate discipline. Advise parents to focus always on the problematic behavior, rather than on the child as the problem.

Parents who used punishment with their child in the past and now attempt to apply discipline measures may find the expected change in their child's behavior to be slow in coming. Children may test their parents more than usual ("Is this real?") or act out in a more extreme way. Prepare parents for this possibility and suggest that, in parenting, slow and consistent changes are best. Giving parents a handout on nonviolent approaches to discipline that can serve as a quick reference is recommended.

Self-Esteem in Children

❑ Rationale

Children are not born with self-esteem; it develops over time as a result of children's interactions with others and personal life experiences. Self-esteem is a combination of one's beliefs and feelings about one's self and one's image of the person one would like to be. A large discrepancy between the perceived self and the ideal self results in low self-esteem.

Self-esteem is recognized as a central factor in good socioemotional adjustment in children and as critically important in their overall functioning (Pope, McHale, & Craighead, 1988). Some evidence suggests that children of battered women have less self-esteem than children from nonviolent homes (Hughes, 1988). This may be a result of a variety of factors, such as feelings of shame and embarrassment about the violence, guilt for not preventing or stopping the violence, and reactive behavioral problems that interfere with schoolwork and social relationships (Jaffe et al., 1990). Hence, parents of child witnesses of violence need to make a conscious effort to support and strengthen their children's self-esteem.

❑ Facilitator Notes and Food for Thought

Acknowledge that parents want what is best for their children: to be happy, to like themselves, and to be successful in their endeavors. Recognize that circumstances beyond the parents' control (e.g., racism, poverty, street violence) can have a negative effect on children's self-esteem. Emphasize that other factors, such as information, insight, and skills, can be learned, developed, and used to help children build positive self-esteem.

Because we cannot give away what we do not have, it is vital that parents be aware of their own self-esteem and work to improve their perceptions of themselves. Suggest that parents can "reparent" themselves by applying to themselves the same ideas and methods they use to support their children's self-esteem.

Children's evaluations of themselves in the areas of academic, social, family, and body image all contribute to their global self-esteem. Discuss ways of enhancing each of these areas of self-esteem. Such work may require parents to change their communication and behavior patterns with their children. Brainstorm with group members about the parental attitudes and behaviors that support and interfere with the development of self-esteem in children. For example, the concepts of *encouragement* and *praise* and the consequences of each in regard to the child's personality and to parent-child relationship can be discussed.

Communication

❏ **Rationale**

Many of the children who live in homes where violence occurs are part of an alliance of silence, keeping the violence as a secret from the outside and, sometimes, from other family members. This silence is a powerful strategy that allows family members to deny and minimize the violence and maintain the status quo. Children learn the rules quickly, even when they are covert or indirect. These rules are, generally, "Don't talk about what happens, don't feel your feelings, don't ask questions, don't challenge the abuser, and above all, don't tell." These rules stifle the natural tendency children have to ask questions in order to make sense of their world and to be open about their feelings.

The purpose of communication is to express what we think and feel and to establish boundaries within our world. Because these goals are actively discouraged in a violent home, children are often profoundly confused and fail to learn healthy communication skills. The result is anger, frustration, and an inability to get their needs met by others around them.

❏ **Facilitator Notes and Food for Thought**

Discuss the strong relationship between family communication patterns and the development of children's self-esteem. Encourage parents to use their roles as "communication models" to benefit their children. Through their own verbal and nonverbal communication, parents can establish new patterns of communication in the family. Open and direct communication offers children a positive message about their worth as human beings and about their place in the world.

Help parents identify their own styles and patterns of verbal and nonverbal communication. Note that 90% of our communication is nonverbal. When relevant and appropriate, make use of communication among group members to explore personal communication patterns. Remember your role as a model of effective communication for group members.

A prerequisite for effective communication is respect and acceptance of the other person's feelings, beliefs, and opinions. Encourage parents to look honestly at their attitudes about their children's beliefs, feelings, and opinions. Exercises can be given to parents to assist them in feeling identification and in developing an awareness of how they typically experience and express their emotions (see Mathews et al., 1990).

Discuss with parents the influence of gender role stereotyping on their communication in general and on their ability to feel and to express feelings in particular. We live in a culture that discourages men from expressing vulnerable and tender feelings and women from expressing anger and strong personal feelings. Examine the influence of these roles on parents' expectations of their children regarding the communication of feelings.

Discuss with parents the concepts of *reflective listening, "I" messages, problem ownership,* and *criticism versus encouragement.* Remind parents that, on the one hand, criticism may discourage children, harm their self-esteem, and leave emotional scars. Encouragement, on the other hand, often motivates children, builds their self-esteem, and contributes to a positive relationship between parent and child.

Sibling Relationships

❏ **Rationale**

Victims/survivors and abusers often report their concerns about their children's hostile, negative, and destructive patterns of interaction with one another. They fear that their children will grow up to repeat the cycle of violence, taking on perpetrator and victim behavior. Reacting out of their own experience of violence, these parents often find it difficult to accurately assess and effectively intervene in sibling fighting.

Victims/survivors may project their own feelings of powerlessness and inadequacy onto their children. Abusers or parents who have a history of battering may intervene in siblings' fights in an aggressive, controlling, or abusive manner, demonstrating further misuse or abuse of power.

Both parents often feel confused about what is "normal" in regard to sibling conflict, fighting, and competition. They often blame themselves for hostile feelings between their children and feel at a loss about what they can do to improve their children's relationships with one another.

❏ **Facilitator Notes and Food for Thought**

Parents' responses to their children's fights do make a difference. Parents are in a position to intensify the fighting or make cooperation possible. This is not to imply that it is an easy task.

Reassure parents that some competitiveness between siblings is common and normal. Because children want exclusive relationships with their parents, they typically bring competitive feelings into their relationships with their siblings. Jealousy is one of the major causes of sibling rivalry, and its extent depends on how secure the children feel about their parents' love. Parents can help their children deal with jealousy and other "bad"

Competitiveness between siblings is both common and normal.

"bad" feelings by encouraging them to express their feelings openly without being judged, criticized, or abused.

Encourage parents to express their own feelings regarding their children. Discuss appropriate and inappropriate expressions of feelings. Validate the existence of different feelings for different children. Suggest that parents seek out the special attributes of a less-favored child and reflect it back to him or her. "Children do not need to be treated equally. They need to be treated uniquely" (Faber & Mazalish, 1987, p. 99). Advise parents not to compare their children, either favorably or unfavorably.

Remind parents that children are born with different personality characteristics, grow at different rates, and may take steps both forward and backward. Each child needs to be treated according to his or her individual best interest. Fairness does not necessarily mean giving equally to each child in terms of gifts, amount of time, or manner in which love is demonstrated. Refer back to the session on self-esteem and challenge parents to decide what each of their children needs for building his or her self-esteem.

Note that behavior is purposeful and that children fight for a reason. Understanding children's motivations is the first step toward eliminating the fighting. Suggest that parents listen to their children's fights in order to understand the motivations (e.g., wanting attention; feeling jealous, unloved, tired, bored, powerless, left out). Brainstorm with parents about effective interventions in their children's fights and work on conflict resolution skills. Remind parents that they do need to step in when one child is being abusive toward another. Encourage parents to bring their challenges back to group as material from which to learn.

Changing Families

❏ **Rationale**

One of every four children in the United States is living with a single parent. One-parent families have become a significant and

---

Box 5.3: Potential Stressors in Separation/Divorce

- Loss of emotional and physical availability of both parents
- Change in household routines
- Decreased economic stability
- Loss of bonds and attachments to neighbors, friends, and family
- Loss of bonds and attachments to familiar objects and spaces
- Having to adjust to new school or caregivers
- Change of role in the family

---

growing presence in our culture: In 1990, 9.7 million families were headed predominantly by women (U.S. Bureau of the Census, 1990).

Unfortunately, our attitudes and beliefs about single-parent families has not caught up with this cultural revolution. Single-parent families are seen as "broken," "deficient," "substandard," and prone to producing children with serious problems. However, it is probably poverty and its accompanying lack of support, hunger, and poor and dangerous neighborhoods that most affect children from female-headed households.

Although living in a single-parent family can be a positive and nurturing experience, initial separation and divorce can be quite stressful for the children. The sources of stress can be directly related to the child (e.g., moving to a new school) or mediated by increased stress for the parent (e.g., mother starts a new job and is less available for the family). Some of these stressors are listed in Box 5.3.

The ways in which children manifest, defend, master, or resolve feelings related to changes in their families involve various factors, including gender, preexisting psychological functioning of the child and the parents, availability of emotional support, the child's repertoire of coping skills, degree of hostility in the parents' relationship, and the child's relationship with each parent. How the family restructures itself and how feelings are handled can have a significant impact on the child's adjustment and continuing growth and development.

❏ **Facilitator Notes and Food for Thought**

No divorce is easy, and no two divorces are alike. Separation, divorce, remarriage, and repartnering usually involve a grieving process for all people involved. Encourage parents to identify their own feelings related to the separation or divorce. Again, we remind parents that they are models for their children and need to share their feelings with them (children will sense parents' feelings, even if hidden). Discuss with parents the difference between sharing feelings with their children and burdening them inappropriately with unresolved feelings.

Provide parents with information about how separation and divorce affect children at different developmental stages. Having realistic expectations is essential for successful coping and healing (Lansky, 1989; Wallerstein & Kelly, 1980). Although general patterns of emotional responses to divorce (guilt, fear, anger, anxiety) have been noted, parents need to pay attention to the individual response of each of their children. Encourage the parents to listen, validate, and accept each child's feelings.

Children need to receive permission for all of their feelings, including anger toward parents and relief that the abusive parent has gone, and to be assured that their parents will not abandon them. If parents are unable to handle their child's feelings, a referral for additional counseling may be required. Encourage parents to check the availability of support resources, such as groups at the child's school.

Parents may need help in learning how to talk with their children about a decision to separate or divorce. Refer parents to public libraries for resources for both parents and children who are responding to divorce. Remind parents that what they say to their child about the other parent, as well as how they say it, affects the child. If a child's parent is criticized or attacked, the child often will feel criticized and attacked.

Children often blame themselves for their parents' separation. Parents need to reassure their children that the separation or divorce was not the children's fault and that they could not have prevented it, no matter what they did. It may be necessary to repeat this message many times before the children actually believe it.

Often, children get caught in the middle of their parents' battles. Parents may need help in understanding what to do to facilitate this process and how to get their children out of the middle. Looking at consequences for the children and for the parent-child relationship may motivate parents to avoid putting their children in the middle. Challenge parents to understand what needs of their own are being met by putting their children in the middle and to learn other ways to meet these needs in a healthy and nonabusive manner.

Significant stressors for parents that may need attention include custody and visitation disputes, ongoing abuse by the ex-partner, lack of financial resources, lack of social support, and depression. Be prepared to provide participants with specific suggestions and recommendations for appropriate referrals.

We remind parents that if an ex-partner continues to behave in a controlling and intimidating manner, then joint decision making regarding the child will be very difficult. Successful coparenting requires that both parents put the best interest of the child first (Pence et al., 1991).

Participants involved in stepfamilies need to understand that the structure of the stepfamily is unique and requires many adjustments by the parents and the children (Einstein & Albert, 1986; Larson, Anderson, & Morgan, 1984). Help parents challenge myths based on misperceptions and stereotypes of stepfamilies. Remind them that making a stepfamily takes time and patience; like divorce, it is not an event, but a process. Note that confusion and chaos are normal stages of this process; this does not imply that their stepfamily is not working.

Conclusion

This chapter provided you with a general framework and major themes for working with parents of child witnesses of domestic violence. The nine topics reviewed are an essential, but not an exhaustive, list of building blocks for healthy and effective parenting in families that have experienced domestic violence.

The tentative parenting group model suggested here is only one component of an effective intervention program with children of battered women. We strongly believe that healing from the direct and indirect effects of violence requires support of both children and their parents, individually and as a family. This integrative perspective directed the children's program presented in this manual.

Appendix A:
Intake and Assessment Forms

This appendix includes all of the forms described in Chapter 3.
Use these forms as part of the child and parent intake and assessment processes. The following are general considerations to keep
in mind when working with these forms:

1. Prepare enough forms before the intake interview.
2. Use clear handwriting so that other people who may need to read the
   completed forms can do so easily.
3. Make sure the names of the child (or the parent) and of the interviewer
   appear on *each* of the forms.
4. Keep all of the forms in one file (e.g., the child's file) for easy accessibility. If you need to transfer some of the forms to another file (e.g., for
   office use), make a copy of these forms for the child's file.
5. Keep a copy of every form you send out (e.g., Release of Information
   Form).

CHILDREN'S SERVICE REQUEST FORM

(sample)

Referring parent's name: _____

Phone number*: _____ Referral source: _____

Other parent's name: _____

Phone number: _____ Referral source: _____

A. Child's name: _____

   Age: _____ D.O.B.: _____ Gender: _____

   Lives with whom? _____ Who has legal custody? _____

   Concerns: _____

   Would you like the child to participate in counseling at

   [agency name]? _____

   yes _____ no _____ maybe _____

B. Child's name: _____

   Age: _____ D.O.B.: _____ Gender: _____

   Lives with whom? _____ Who has legal custody? _____

   Concerns: _____

   Would you like the child to participate in counseling at

   [agency name]? _____

   yes _____ no _____ maybe _____

*If you have an answering machine or if you are not at home, is it okay to leave a message?

yes _____ no _____

PHONE INTERVIEW FORM

Date: _____ Name of interviewer: _____

Name of parent/guardian interviewed: _____

Address: _____

_____

Phone: (H) _____   (W) _____

Child Information

(Fill separately for each intake candidate)

A. Child's name: _____

   Age: _____   D.O.B.: _____   Gender: _____

   Lives with whom? _____

   Who has legal custody? _____

   If child is living out of home, plans for near-future living
   arrangements and available social and family support: _____

   _____

   _____

   Concerns and/or problems (including possible causes/
   explanations):

   _____

   _____

   _____

   Special needs: _____

   _____

B. Child's name: _____

    Age: _____   D.O.B.: _____   Gender: _____

    Lives with whom? _____ Who has legal custody? _____

    If child is living out of home, plans for near-future living
    arrangements and available social and family support: _____

    _____

    _____

    Concerns and/or problems (including possible causes/
    explanations):

    _____

    _____

    _____

    Special needs: _____

    _____

C. Child's name: _____

    Age: _____   D.O.B.: _____   Gender: _____

    Lives with whom? _____ Who has legal custody? _____

    If child is living out of home, plans for near-future living
    arrangements and available social and family support: _____

    _____

    _____

    Concerns and/or problems (including possible causes/
    explanations):

    _____

    _____

    _____

    Special needs: _____

    _____

Parent Information

Parent's family violence counseling (dates, agency, and completion status):

    Individual: _____

    Couple: _____

    Family: _____

    Group: _____

Partner's family violence counseling (dates, agency, and completion status):

    Individual: _____

    Couple: _____

    Family: _____

    Group: _____

Current relationship status: _____

Current relationship situation with abusive partner (including child's exposure to violence): _____

_____

_____

Is the abusive partner the child's other parent?   yes _____   no _____

Involvement of abusive partner in the child's life: _____

_____

Abusive partner's support of child's group participation: _____

_____

_____

Do you think the involvement of the abusive partner in the intake process would compromise in any way your safety or the safety of your child? Explain: _____

_____

_____

_____

Interviewed parent gave consent for contacting other parent:
        yes _____   no _____

Other parent's name: _____ Phone: _____

Comments: _____

_____

_____

_____

_____

_____

_____

_____

Intake scheduled: yes _____   no _____

Intake date: _____ Intake counselor: _____

Outside referral: _____

PERMISSION TO TREAT MINORS FORM

(sample)

Permission to Treat Minors

(Fill out one form for each child)

I give the

_____

Agency name

permission to provide assessment and counseling services for my minor child.

_____

Child's name

Because

_____

Agency name

is identified as a helping professional, all employees are mandated reporters. Therefore, if a therapist knows or has reason to believe that my child has been or is being physically abused, sexually abused, or neglected, I understand that this information must be reported to Child Protection Services.

I also understand that the specific content of sessions between my child and his/her therapist will remain confidential and that my child has the right to request that information about his/her treatment not be shared with me.

(However, all information concerning danger to my child will be reported. General reports of my child's progress also may be made to me under this agreement.)

_____

Signature of parent with legal custody

_____

Date

RELEASE OF INFORMATION FORM

(sample)

TO: _____

RE: _____

I authorize you to release the following information from my child's
treatment records to

_____

Agency name

(Indicate with YES or NO):

_____ Narrative account of case history, diagnosis, progress and
recommendations for future programs of counseling.

_____ Psychological testing results.

_____ Phone contact.

_____ Other: _____

_____ I also authorize

_____

Agency name

to disclose to the above-named person any information
pertinent to participation in my child's treatment program.

I understand this disclosure will be used for the purpose of receiving
therapeutic services for my child at

_____

Agency name

This release will expire one year from the date signed unless I revoke
it sooner in writing.

_____   _____
Parent or Legal Guardian   Date

_____   _____
Minor Client Signature   Date

_____   _____
Counselor Signature   Date

DEVELOPMENTAL INFORMATION FORM

(Filled out by parent)

Date: _____ Child's name: _____

Child's gender: _____ Child's age _____ D.O.B.: _____

Parent's name (specify if other relationship to child): _____

1. How was the pregnancy and delivery of this child?

   Normal _____   Complications _____

   Describe: _____

2. Was there physical abuse during pregnancy? Describe: _____

   _____

3. Did early developmental stages (walking alone, first words, toilet training) occur on time? yes _____   no_____

   If not, explain: _____

   _____

4. How is your child's health?

   Excellent _____   Good _____   Poor _____

5. Where does your child receive health care? _____

   Doctor _____ Phone _____

6. Has your child had any of the following problems with health?

   _____ Unconscious   Describe: _____

   _____ Seizures   Describe: _____

   _____ Head injuries   Describe: _____

   _____ High or prolonged fever   Describe: _____

   What is the child's most frequent health problem? _____

   _____

   _____

   _____

7. Describe any accidents or serious illnesses your child has had: __

_____

_____

_____

8. Is your child taking any medications? yes _____   no_____

   What kind and why? _____

9. Have you noticed any of the following changes in behavior recently or when child was under stress?

   _____ Withdrawing   ___ Bed wetting

   _____ Fears   ___ Crying, whining

   _____ Concentration problems   ___ Harms self

   _____ Eating or appetite problems   ___ Destruction of property

   _____ Temper outbursts   ___ Sleeping problems

   _____ Yelling   ___ Missing school

10. What school is your child currently attending? _____

    Grade: _____   Is your child receiving any special assistance at school, such as tutoring, advanced placements, or special classes?
                  yes ____   no_____

    Describe: _____

    _____

11. Why have you decided to bring your child to

    _____

    Agency name

    _____

    _____

PARENT INTERVIEW FORM

(Filled out by counselor)

Date: _____ Name of counselor: _____

Name of parent (specify relationship with child if other than parent):

_____

Name of child: _____

Preinterview Counselor Checklist

[ ] The parent is informed on the agency's philosophy and programs.

[ ] The parent understands intake procedures.

[ ] Issues of confidentiality and mandatory reporting were discussed, and the parent has signed a Permission to Treat Minors Form.

Family Relationships

1. Who is in your family (name, age, gender)? _____

_____

_____

_____

2. Who lives in your household (name, age, and gender, if different from above)? _____

_____

_____

_____

3. What is your current relationship status (legal, living arrangements) from the child's other parent? _____

_____

_____

_____

4. Are you divorced or separated from the child's other parent?

   yes _____   no _____

   When did you separate/divorce?_____

   How old was your child at the time? _____

5. Does your partner/ex-partner have visitation and does he/she consistently use this privilege? _____

   Are these arrangements suitable for your child? Explain: _____

   _____

6. Describe your child's relationship with your ex-partner: _____

   _____

   _____

7. Describe your current partner's relationship with your child: ___

   _____

   _____

8. Describe your relationship with your child: _____

   _____

   _____

9. Describe your child's relationships with his/her siblings: _____

   _____

   _____

10. How is affection shown in your family? _____

    _____

    _____

11. How is anger shown in your family? _____

    _____

    _____

Child Behavior and Relationships

12. How would you describe your child's main characteristics? (include strengths and weaker areas) _____

_____

_____

13. Regarding the following, how do you know when your child is:

    afraid: _____

    _____

    angry: _____

    _____

    physically hurt: _____

    _____

    sad: _____

    _____

    feels fine: _____

    _____

14. How does your child resolve conflicts with other family members?

    _____

    _____

    _____

15. How would you describe your child's relationship with friends/peers (ages of peers, follower, leader, extrovert, introvert)? ____

    _____

    _____

    _____

16. How does your child resolve conflict with peers (negotiates, withdraws, yells, hits)? _____

    _____

    _____

17. Tell me about the way your child plays (what types of activities, plays alone, with others): _____

_____

_____

18. Tell me about your child's school performance (academic achievements and problems): _____

_____

_____

Parenting

19. How have you disciplined your child over the course of his/her development? _____

_____

_____

_____

_____

20. How did your ex-partner discipline your child over the course of the child's development? _____

_____

_____

21. How does your current partner discipline your child? (Include changes over time if relevant.) _____

_____

_____

22. If anything, what would you like to change about the way you parent?

_____

_____

_____

Violence Directed at Child

23. Do you have any suspicions or concerns that your child has been sexually touched or abused? (possible indicators: sexual symptoms, somatic symptoms with sexual content, physical signs, paternal jealousy, running away and prostitution, child's verbal report)

    yes _____   no _____

    Why (indicators)? _____

    _____

    By whom? _____ When? _____

    Where? _____

    Child's reaction? _____

    _____

24. Do you have any suspicions or concerns that your child has been physically abused (grabbed, pushed, pinched, hair pulled, punched, spanked, kicked, slapped, hit with object, thrown)?

    yes _____   no _____

    Describe abusive behavior: _____

    _____

    By whom? _____ Where? _____

    When (including last time)? _____

    Child's reaction: _____

    _____

25. Do you have any suspicions or concerns that your child has been emotionally abused? (threatened, called names, put down)

    yes _____   no _____

    Describe abusive behavior: _____

    _____

    By whom? _____

    Where (e.g., public place, in front of friends)? _____

When (including last time)? _____

Child's reaction: _____

_____

26. Has Child Protection Services intervened with your child?

yes _____   no _____

Reasons for involvement: _____

_____

Type of services provided: _____

_____

What requirements has CPS imposed on the parents? _____

_____

Dates of involvement: _____ County: _____

Worker: _____ Phone: _____

27. Has your child been involved in counseling or family violence program before?

yes _____   no _____

I.   Agency: _____

Counselor: _____

Dates: _____

Description of intervention: _____

_____

Was it helpful? How? _____

_____

II. Agency: _____

Counselor: _____

Dates: _____

Description of intervention: _____

_____

Was it helpful? How? _____

_____

28. Do you have any concerns that your child is self-injurious or that he/she is likely to hurt himself/herself (e.g., cutting self with sharp objects, pulling own hair, banging own head against a solid object, scratching oneself)?

yes _____   no _____

Explain: _____

_____

_____

Violence Witnessed by Child

29. Describe abusive behavior that has occurred between you and your partner since your child's birth (type, frequency, severity, child's age):

_____

_____

_____

30. Describe the most memorable incidents of violence between you and your partner that your child has heard or witnessed (If witnessing was frequent, describe typical incidents):

I. Abused witnessed: _____

_____

Abuser: _____ When (child's age)? _____

Where? _____

Child's response (verbal and behavioral): _____

_____

_____

II. Abused witnessed: _____

_____

Abuser: _____ When (child's age)? _____

Where? _____

Child's response (verbal and behavioral): _____

_____

_____

31. Have you talked with your child about the violence/abuse in your family?

    yes _____   no _____

    Explain: _____

    _____

    _____

32. How do you think your child has been affected by the violence/abuse in your family? _____

    _____

    _____

33. Has your child witnessed any other violent and/or abusive events inside or outside the family (e.g., incest, sibling abuse, gang violence)?

    yes _____   no _____

    Describe: _____

    _____

    _____

34. Beyond violence, has your child experienced any traumatic events throughout his/her life (e.g., a death, injury, separation)?

    yes _____   no _____

    Describe: _____

    _____

    _____

Summary

35. What do you think will be most helpful in dealing with the concerns you raised about your child? _____

   _____

   _____

   _____

36. Is there anything else about your child that may be helpful for us to know? _____

   _____

   _____

   _____

Do you have any questions?

Interviewer Comments/Observations

_____

_____

_____

_____

_____

_____

_____

_____

_____

_____

_____

CHILD INTAKE FORM (ages 4-6)

Date: _____ Name of counselor: _____

Name of child: _____

Age: _____ D.O.B.: _____

Name of parent (specify relationship with child if other than parent):

_____

Preinterview Counselor Checklist

[ ] The child understands intake procedures.

[ ] Issues of confidentiality and mandatory reporting were discussed with the child.

Introduction

1. How did you feel about coming here today? (Interviewer can engage in a short conversation about how other children often feel—for example, scared because they don't know what is going to happen, bad because they think they did something wrong.)

_____

_____

School

2. (For ages 4 to 5) Do you go to day care/preschool? _____

3. What do you like best about your day care/preschool/school? __

_____

_____

Interpersonal Relationships (Friends)

4. Do you have friends to play with at day care/preschool/kindergarten?

_____

Do you have friends to play with at home? _____

_____

5. What do you like to do with your friends? _____

_____

6. What do you do when you get mad at your friends? _____

_____

Interpersonal Relationships (Family)

7. Tell me the names of everyone in your family: _____

_____

8. Who lives at home with you? _____

_____

9. Where does everyone sleep? _____

_____

10. Who in your family do you like to be with a lot? _____

_____

11. When you feel worried, sad, or scared, who in your family do
you talk to? _____

_____

Do they help you? _____

12. Is there anyone in your family you don't like to be with
sometimes? (If yes, explore who and why.) _____

_____

Self-Concept

13. Name two things you like about yourself or that you are good at:

_____

_____

_____

Feeling States

14. What is the happiest time you remember? _____

   _____

15. What is the scariest thing that happened to you? _____

   _____

16. What did you do when you got scared? _____

   _____

17. What is the saddest thing that ever happened to you? _____

   _____

18. What sorts of things do you get mad about? _____

   _____

19. What do you do when you get really mad? _____

   _____

Child Abuse

20. When you break something at home or don't do what your mom
   and/or dad (or mom's partner) tell you to do, what happens?

   _____

   _____

21. Some children tell me they get touched in private places on their
   body by people who are close to them, like someone in their
   family, or even by people they don't know. Has anything like
   this ever happened to you? (Explore who, when, where, how, if
   he/she ever told anyone, and associated feelings.) _____

   _____

   _____

   _____

22. Some children tell me they get hurt in other ways, like getting slapped, pushed, or hit by people in their family (mom, dad, sister, brother) or by other people (baby-sitter, neighbor, relative, etc.). Has anything like this ever happened to you? (Explore who, when, where, how, if he/she ever told anyone, and associated feelings.) _____

   _____

   _____

   _____

23. **Body Diagram:** Give a green and a red crayon to the child and invite him/her to pretend that this is a picture of him/her. You can draw a face on one diagram to represent the front of the body and hair on the head of the other diagram to represent the child's back side. Children like it when the face and hair resemble their own.

    Ask the child to use the green crayon to color all the places on his/her body (front and back) that were touched in a way he/she liked. You can coach the child if he/she does not seem to understand (e.g., someone combed your hair, rubbed your back and shoulders).

    Then ask the child to use the red crayon to color all the places on his/her body (front and back) that were touched in a way that didn't feel good or that was confusing. You can coach the child by repeating information he/she may have revealed earlier in the interview (e.g., fighting with siblings). Be sure to make written explanations for all markings on the body diagram, including who, when, and where (see sample body diagram at the end of this form).

Violence Witnessed by the Child

24. We know that fighting happens in a lot of families. All of the children who come here have heard or seen their parents (or mom and her partner/boyfriend) fight. Can you tell me what you remember about the fighting? _____

    _____

    _____

25. What do you do when they fight? _____

_____

26. How do you feel when they fight? _____

_____

27. Why do you think they fight? _____

_____

28. Some children tell me they think the fighting is their fault.
    Have you ever thought this before? (Explore further. Remind the
    child that the fighting is not his/her fault.) _____

_____

29. Do your brothers or sisters ever get hurt? (Explore who, how,
    and when was the last time.) _____

_____

We are almost finished. I have a few fun questions to ask you, and
then you can ask me any questions.

Fantasy

30. Sometimes it's fun to pretend we're an animal. If you could be an
    animal, what would you be? _____

    Why? _____

31. Let's pretend you could have three wishes. What would you
    wish for? (Coach the child if necessary: Is there anything you
    wish were different for you at home, in school, etc.)

    1. _____

    2. _____

    3. _____

Conclusion

32. Do you have any questions for me, or is there anything you are wondering about? _____

_____

Interviewer Comments/Observations

_____

_____

_____

_____

Body Diagram

Date: _____ Interviewer: _____

Child's name: _____

Age: _____   D.O.B.: _____

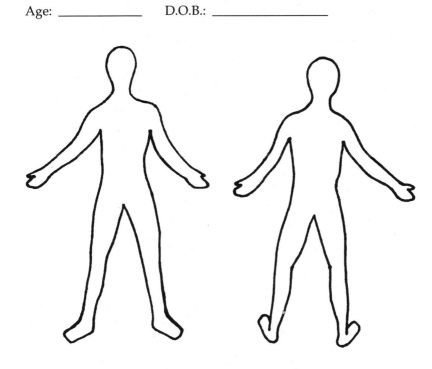

CHILD INTAKE FORM (ages 7-9)

Date: _____ Name of counselor: _____

Name of child: _____

Age: _____   D.O.B.: _____

Name of parent (specify relationship with child if other than parent):

_____

Preinterview Counselor Checklist

[ ] The child understands intake procedures.

[ ] Issues of confidentiality and mandatory reporting were discussed with the child.

Introduction

1. How did you feel about coming here today? (Interviewer can engage in a short conversation about how other children often feel—for example, scared because they don't know what is going to happen, bad because they think they did something wrong.)

_____

_____

_____

School

2. Which school do you go to? _____

3. What is your teacher's name? _____

4. What do you like best about your school? _____

5. Is there anything you don't like about school? _____

Interpersonal Relationships (Friends)

6. Do you have friends to play with at school? _____

Do you have friends to play with at home? _____

7. Do you have a best friend? _____

8. What do you like to do with your best friend? _____

9. What do you do when you get mad at your best friend or one
   of your other friends? _____

10. Do you ever play by yourself? _____

    What do you like to do? _____

    _____

Interpersonal Relationships (Family)

11. Tell me the names of everyone in your family: _____

    _____

12. Who lives at home with you? _____

    _____

13. Where does everyone sleep? _____

    _____

14. What do you like to do with your family? _____

    _____

15. Who in your family do you like to be with a lot? _____

    _____

16. When you feel worried, sad, or scared, who in your family do
    you tell it to? _____

    _____

    Do they help you? _____

17. Is there anyone in your family you don't like to be with
    sometimes? (If yes, explore who and why.) _____

    _____

Self-Concept

18. Name two things you like about yourself or that you are good at:

_____

_____

19. If you could be any age at all, what age would you be and why?

_____

_____

Feeling States

20. What is the happiest time you remember? _____

_____

21. What is the scariest thing that happened to you? _____

_____

22. What did you do when you got scared? _____

_____

23. What is the saddest thing that ever happened to you? _____

_____

24. What sorts of things do you get mad about? _____

_____

25. What do you do when you get really mad? _____

_____

Child Abuse

26. When you break something at home or don't do what your mom and/or dad (or mom's partner) tells you to do, what happens?

_____

_____

27. Some children tell me they get touched in private places on their body by people who are close to them, like someone in their family, or even by people they don't know. Has anything like this ever happened to you? (Explore who, when, where, how, if he/she ever told anyone, and associated feelings.)

_____

_____

_____

_____

28. Some children tell me they get hurt in other ways, like getting slapped, pushed, or hit by people in their family (mom, dad, sister, brother) or by other people (baby-sitter, neighbor, relative, etc.). Has anything like this ever happened to you? (Explore who, when, where, how, if he/she ever told anyone, and associated feelings.)

_____

_____

_____

_____

29. **Body Diagram:** Give a green and a red crayon to the child and invite him/her to pretend this is a picture of him/her. You can draw a faceon one diagram to represent the front of the body and hair on the head of the other diagram to represent the child's back side. Children like it when the face and hair resemble their own.

Ask the child to use the green crayon to color all the places on his/her body (front and back) that were touched in a way he/she liked. You can coach the child if he/she does not seem to understand (e.g., someone combed your hair, rubbed your back and shoulders).

Then ask the child to use the red crayon to color all the places on his/her body (front and back) that were touched in a way that didn't feel good or that was confusing. You can coach the child by repeating information he/she may have revealed earlier in the interview (e.g., fighting with siblings). Be sure to make written explanations for all markings on the body diagram, including who, when, and where (see sample body diagram at the end of this form).

Violence Witnessed by the Child

30. We know that fighting happens in a lot of families. All of the children who come here have heard or seen their parents (or mom and her partner/boyfriend) fight. Can you tell me what you remember about the fighting? _____

_____

_____

31. What do you do when they fight? _____

_____

32. How do you feel when they fight? _____

_____

33. Why do you think they fight? _____

_____

34. Some children tell me they think the fighting is their fault. Have you ever thought this before? (Explore further. Remind the child that the fighting is not his/her fault.) _____

_____

35. Do your brothers or sisters ever get hurt? (Explore who, how, and when was the last time.) _____

_____

We are almost finished. I have a few fun questions to ask you, and then you can ask me any questions.

Fantasy

36. Sometimes it's fun to pretend we're an animal. If you could be an animal, what would you be? _____

Why? _____

37. Let's pretend you could have three wishes. What would you wish for? (Coach the child if necessary: Is there anything that you wish was different for you at home, in school, etc.)

1. _____

2. _____

3. _____

Conclusion

38. Do you have any questions for me, or is there anything you are wondering about? _____

_____

_____

Interviewer Comments/Observations

_____

_____

_____

_____

_____

_____

_____

_____

_____

_____

Body Diagram

Date: _____ Interviewer: _____

Child's name: _____

Age: _____   D.O.B.: _____

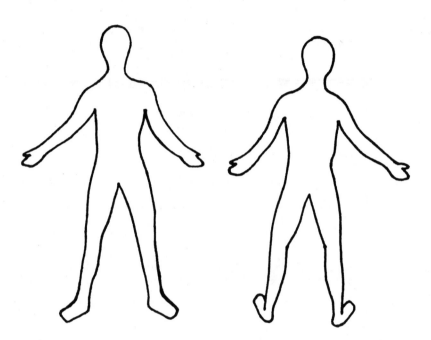

CHILD INTAKE FORM (ages 10-12)

Date: _____ Name of counselor: _____

Name of child: _____

Age: _____ D.O.B.: _____

Name of parent (specify relationship with child if other than parent):

_____

Preinterview Counselor Checklist

[ ] The child understands intake procedures.

[ ] Issues of confidentiality and mandatory reporting were discussed with the child.

Introduction

1. How did you feel about coming here today? (Interviewer can engage in a short conversation about how other children often feel—for example, scared because they don't know what is going to happen, bad because they think they did something wrong.)

_____

_____

2. Why do you think your parent(s) brought you here? _____

_____

School

3. Which school do you go to? _____

4. How do you like your teachers? _____

5. What do you like best about school? _____

6. Is there anything you don't like about school? _____

_____

7. Have you changed schools in the past year? _____

(if yes) How did you feel about it? _____

_____

8. What do you do after school? _____

Interpersonal Relationships (Friends)

9. Do you have friends at school? _____

Do you have friends in your neighborhood? _____

10. Do you have a best friend? _____

11. What do you like to do with your best friend or with other friends?

_____

12. Do you like to be alone at times? _____

What do you like to do when you're alone? _____

13. What happens when you don't get along with your friends? __

_____

Interpersonal Relationships (Family)

14. Tell me the names of everyone in your family: _____

_____

15. Is everyone living at home? ____ If not, where do the others live?

_____

How often do you see them? _____

Are these arrangements okay with you? _____

If not, why? _____

16. What do you like to do with your family? _____

_____

17. Who in your family do you like to be with a lot? _____

_____

18. Is there anyone in your family you don't like to be with sometimes? (If yes, explore who and why.) _____

_____

19. If you could change anything about your family, what would you change? _____

_____

_____

Self-Concept

20. Name two things you like about yourself or that you are good at:

_____

_____

21. If you could change anything about yourself, what would you change? (Therapist can coach if necessary.) _____

_____

22. If you could be any age, what age would you be and why? ___

_____

Feeling States

23. What is the happiest time you remember? _____

_____

24. What is the scariest thing that happened to you? _____

_____

    What did you do when you got scared? _____

_____

25. What is the saddest thing that ever happened to you? _____

_____

26. When you feel sad, does it ever last for a long time? (Explore further.) _____

_____

27. What sorts of things do you get mad about? _____

_____

28. What do you do when you get really mad? _____

_____

29. Have you ever thought of hurting yourself? (Explore further. When was the last time, how would you hurt yourself, who else knows about this, do you feel this way now?) _____

_____

_____

_____

Child Abuse

30. When you break something at home or don't do what your mom and/or dad (or mom's partner) tell you to do, what happens? _____

_____

31. Some children tell me they get touched in private places on their body by people who are close to them, like someone in their family, or even by people they don't know. Has anything like this ever happened to you? (Explore who, when, where, how, if he/she ever told anyone, and associated feelings.) _____

_____

_____

32. Some children tell me they get hurt in other ways, like getting slapped, pushed, or hit by people in their family (mom, dad, sister, brother) or by other people (baby-sitter, neighbor, relative, etc.). Hasanything like this ever happened to you? (Explore who, when, where, how, if he/she ever told anyone, associated feelings.)

_____

_____

_____

_____

33. **Body Diagram:** Give a green and a red crayon to the child and invite him/her to pretend this is a picture of him/her. You can draw a face on one diagram to represent the front of the body and hair on the head of the other diagram to represent the child's back side. Children like it when the face and hair resemble their own.

Ask the child to use the green crayon to color all the places on his/her body (front and back) that were touched in a way he/she liked. You can coach the child if he/she does not seem to understand (e.g., someone combed your hair, rubbed your back and shoulders).

Then ask the child to use the red crayon to color all the places on his/her body (front and back) that were touched in a way that didn't feel good or that was confusing. You can coach the child by repeating information he/she may have revealed earlier in the interview (e.g., fighting with siblings). Be sure to make written explanations for all markings on the body diagram, including who, when, and where (see body diagram at the end of this form).

Violence Witnessed by the Child

34. We know that fighting happens in a lot of families. All of the children who come here have heard or seen their parents (or mom and her partner/boyfriend) fight. Can you tell me what you remember about the fighting? _____

_____

_____

35. What do you do when they fight? _____

_____

36. How do you feel when they fight? _____

_____

37. Why do you think they fight? _____

_____

38. Some children tell me they think the fighting is their fault. Have you ever thought this before? (Explore further. Remind the child that the fighting is not his/her fault.) _____

_____

39. Do your brothers or sisters ever get hurt? (Explore who, how, and when was the last time.) _____

_____

We are almost finished. I have a few fun questions to ask you, and then you can ask me any questions.

Fantasy

40. Pretend you are an animal. If you could be an animal, what would you be? _____

    Why? _____

41. Pretend you could have three wishes. What would you wish for? (Coach the child if necessary: Is there anything you wish was different for you at home, in school, etc.)

    1. _____

    2. _____

    3. _____

Conclusion

42. Do you have any questions for me, or is there anything you are wondering about? _____

_____

_____

Interviewer Comments/Observations

_____

_____

_____

_____

_____

_____

_____

_____

Body Diagram

Date: _____ Interviewer: _____

Child's name: _____

Age: _____   D.O.B.: _____

Appendix B:
Desired Outcomes Evaluation Form

DESIRED OUTCOMES EVALUATION FORM

(sample)

Date: _____ Counselor's name: _____

Child's name: _____ Age: _____

ORIENTATION

Desired Outcomes for Child and Parent

1. Is the child familiar with agency, staff, and program?

   [ ] yes   [ ] no   [ ] partially   [ ] not sure

Evidence: _____

_____

Comments: _____

_____

2. Does the child wish to participate in group?

   [ ] yes   [ ] no   [ ] maybe   [ ] not sure

Evidence: _____

_____

Comments: _____

_____

General comments: _____

_____

_____

_____

References

Achenbach, T. M., & Edelbrock, C. (1983). *Manual for the Child Behavior Checklist and Revised Child Behavior Checklist.* Burlington: University of Vermont.

Alesi, J. J., & Hearn, K. (1984). Group treatment of children in shelters for battered women. In A. R. Roberts (Ed.), *Battered women and their families* (pp. 49-61). New York: Springer.

American Psychiatric Association. *Diagnostic and Statistical Manual* (4th ed.) (*DSM-IV*). (1994). Washington, DC: Author.

Arroyo, W., & Eth, S. (1995). Assessment following violence-witnessing trauma. In E. Peled, P. G. Jaffe, & J. L. Edleson (Eds.), *Ending the cycle of violence: Community responses to children of battered women* (pp. 27-42). Thousand Oaks, CA: Sage.

Besharov, D. J. (1990). *Recognizing child abuse: A guide for the concerned.* New York: Free Press.

Bierman, C. L. (1990). Using the clinical interview to assess children's interpersonal reasoning and emotional understanding. In C. R. Reynolds & R. W. Kamphaus (Eds.), *Handbook of psychological and educational assessment of children* (pp. 204-219). New York: Guilford.

Bilinkoff, J. (1995). Empowering battered women as mothers. In E. Peled, P. G. Jaffe, & J. L. Edleson (Eds.), *Ending the cycle of violence: Community responses to children of battered women* (pp. 97-105). Thousand Oaks, CA: Sage.

Black, D., & Kaplan, T. (1988). Father kills mother: Issues and problems encountered by a child psychiatric team. *British Journal of Psychiatry, 153,* 624-630.

Brassard, M. R., Germain, R., & Hart, S. N. (Eds.). (1983). *Psychological maltreatment of children and youth.* New York: Pergamon.

Brygger, M. P., & Edleson, J. L. (1987). The Domestic Abuse Project: A multi-systems intervention in woman battering. *Journal of Interpersonal Violence, 3,* 324-336.

Butler, S. (1986). *Everyone's a winner! Noncompetitive games for people of all ages.* Minneapolis: Bethany House.

Carlson, B. E. (1984). Children's observations of interparental violence. In A. R. Roberts (Ed.), *Battered women and their families* (pp. 147-167). New York: Springer.

Carlson, B. E. (1990). Adolescent observers of marital violence. *Journal of Family Violence, 5,* 285-299.

Cassady, L., Allen, B., Lyon, E., & McGeehan, C. (1987, July). *The Child-Focused Intervention Program: Program evaluation for children in a battered women's shelter.* Paper presented at the Third National Family Violence Researchers Conference, Durham, NH.

Christopherpoulos, C., Cohn, A. D., Shaw, D. S., Joyce, S., Sullivan-Hanson, J., Kraft, S. P., & Emery, R. E. (1987). Children of abused women: I. Adjustment at time of shelter residence. *Journal of Marriage and the Family, 49,* 611-619.

Davies, D. (1991). Intervention with male toddlers who have witnessed parental violence. *Families in Society: The Journal of Contemporary Human Services, 72,* 515-524.

Davis, D. (1984). *Something is wrong at my house: A book about parents fighting.* Seattle: Parenting Press.

Davis, L. V., & Carlson, B. E. (1987). Observations of spouse abuse: What happens to the children? *Journal of Interpersonal Violence, 2,* 278-291.

Diamond, C. B. (1988). General issues in the clinical assessment of children and adolescents. In C. J. Kestenbaum & D. T. Williams (Eds.), *Handbook of clinical assessment of children and adolescents* (pp. 43-55). New York: New York University Press.

Dinkmeyer, D., & McKay, G. (1989). *STEP: The parent's handbook.* Circle Pines, MN: AGS.

Dobash, R. E., & Dobash, R. (1979). *Violence against wives.* New York: Free Press.

Domestic Abuse Project. (1993). *Women's program manual.* Minneapolis: Author.

Dubowitz, H. (1986). *Child maltreatment in the United States: Etiology, impact, and prevention.* Background paper prepared for the Congress of the United States, Office of Technology Assessment.

Dutton, M. A. (1992). *Empowering and healing the battered woman.* New York: Springer.

Echlin, C., & Marshall, L. (1995). Child protection services for children of battered women: Practice and controversy. In E. Peled, P. G. Jaffe, & J. L. Edleson (Eds.), *Ending the cycle of violence: Community responses to children of battered women* (pp. 170-185). Thousand Oaks, CA: Sage.

Edleson, J. L. (1991). Social workers' intervention in women abuse: A study of case records from 1907 to 1945. *Social Service Review, 65,* 304-313.

Edleson, J. L., & Tolman, R. M. (1992). *Intervention for men who batter: An ecological approach.* Newbury Park, CA: Sage.

Einstein, E., & Albert, L. (1986). *Strengthening your stepfamily.* Circle Pines, MN: AGS.

Elbow, M. (1982). Children of violent marriage: The forgotten victim. *Social Casework, 8,* 465-468.

Faber, A., & Mazalish, E. (1987). *Siblings without rivalry: How to help your children live together so you can live too.* New York: Avon.

Fantuzzo, J. W., DePaola, L. M., Lambert, L., Martino, T., Anderson, G., & Sutton, S. (1991). Effects of interparental violence on the psychological adjustment and competencies of young children. *Journal of Consulting and Clinical Psychology, 59,* 258-265.

Federal Child Abuse Prevention and Treatment Act of 1974, 42 U.C.C. 5102(1) (Supp. 1989).

Forsstrom-Cohn, B., & Rosenbaum, A. (1985). The effects of parental marital violence on young adults: An exploratory investigation. *Journal of Marriage and the Family, 47,* 467-472.

Ganley, A. L. (1987). Perpetrators of domestic violence: An overview of counseling the court-mandated client. In D. J. Sonkin (Ed.), *Domestic violence on trial: Psychological and legal dimensions of family violence* (pp. 155-173). New York: Springer.

Garbarino, J., Dubrow, N., Kostelny, K., & Pardo, C. (1992). *Children in danger: Coping with the consequences of community violence.* San Francisco: Jossey-Bass.

Garbarino, J., Guttmann, E., & Seeley, J. W. (1986). *The psychologically battered child: Strategies for identification, assessment, and intervention.* San Francisco: Jossey-Bass.

Gentry, C. E., & Eaddy, V. B. (1980). Treatment of children in spouse abusive families. *Victimology, 2-4,* 240-250.

Gibson, J. W., & Gutierrez, L. (1991). A service program for safe-home children. *Families in Society: The Journal of Contemporary Human Services, 72,* 554-562.

Gil, E. (1991). *The healing power of play: Working with abused children.* New York: Guilford.

Gilgun, J. F. (1989). Freedom of choice and research interviewing in child sexual abuse. In B. G. Compton & B. Gallaway (Eds.), *Social work processes* (4th ed., pp. 358-369). Homewood, IL: Dorsey.

Goolkasian, G. A. (1986). *Confronting domestic violence: A guide for criminal justice agencies.* Washington, DC: U.S. Department of Justice, National Institute of Justice.

Gordon, L. (1988). *Heroes of their own life: The politics and history of family violence— Boston 1880-1960.* New York: Viking.

Greenspan, S. I., & Greenspan, N. T. (1991). *The clinical interview of the child.* Washington, DC: American Psychiatric Press.

Grusznski, R. J., Brink, J. C., & Edleson, J. L. (1988). Support and education groups for children of battered women. *Child Welfare, 68,* 431-444.

Gyrch, J. H., & Fincham, F. D. (1990). Marital conflict and children's adjustment: A cognitive-contextual framework. *Psychological Bulletin, 108,* 267-290.

Haugaard, J. J., & Reppucci, N. D. (1988). *The sexual abuse of children.* San Francisco: Jossey-Bass.

Hendricks, G., & Wills, R. (1975). *The centering book: Awareness activities for children and adults to relax the body and mind.* Englewood Cliffs, NJ: Prentice Hall.

Hilberman, E., & Munson, K. (1977-1978). Sixty battered women. *Victimology, 2,* 460-471.

Hinchey, F. S., & Gavelek, J. R. (1982). Empathic responding in children of battered women. *Child Abuse and Neglect, 6,* 395-401.

Holden, G. W., & Ritchie, K. L. (1991). Linking extreme marital discord, child rearing, and child behavior problems: Evidence from battered women. *Child Development, 62,* 311-327.

Holtzworth-Munroe, A., & Arias, I. (1993). The influence of values in the treatment of marital violence. *Family Violence and Sexual Assault Bulletin, 9*(3), 22-25.

Hotaling, G. T., & Straus, M. A., with Lincoln, A. J. (1989). Intrafamily violence, and crime and violence outside the family. In L. Ohlin & M. Tonry (Eds.), *Family violence* (pp. 315-376). Chicago: University of Chicago Press.

Hughes, H. M. (1982). Brief interventions with children in a battered women's shelter: A model preventive program. *Family Relations, 31,* 495-502.

Hughes, H. M. (1988). Psychological and behavioral correlates of family violence in child witnesses and victims. *American Journal of Orthopsychiatry, 58,* 77-90.

Hughes, H. M., & Barad, S. J. (1983). Psychological functioning of children in battered women's shelter: A preliminary investigation. *American Journal of Orthopsychiatry, 53,* 525-531.

Hughes, H. M., & Marshall, M. (1995). Advocacy for children of battered women. In E. Peled, P. G. Jaffe, & J. L. Edleson (Eds.), *Ending the cycle of violence: Community responses to children of battered women* (pp. 121-144). Thousand Oaks, CA: Sage.

Hughes, H. M., Parkinson, D., & Vargo, M. (1989). Witnessing spouse abuse and experiencing physical abuse: A "double whammy"? *Journal of Family Violence, 4,* 197-209.

Hughes, H. M., Vargo, M. C., Ito, E. S., & Skinner, S. K. (1991). Psychological adjustment of children of battered women: Influences of gender. *Family Violence Bulletin, 7,* 15-17.

Jaffe, P., Wilson, S., & Wolfe, D. A. (1986). Promoting changes in attitudes and understanding of conflict among child witnesses of family violence. *Canadian Journal of Behavioral Science, 18,* 356-380.

Jaffe, P., Wolfe, D. A., & Wilson, S. (1990). *Children of battered women.* Newbury Park, CA: Sage.

Jaffe, P., Wolfe, D. A., Wilson, S., & Zak, L. (1986a). Family violence and child adjustment: A comparative analysis of girls' and boys' behavioral symptoms. *American Journal of Psychiatry, 143,* 74-76.

Jaffe, P., Wolfe, D. A., Wilson, S., & Zak, L. (1986b). Similarities in behavioral and social maladjustment among child victims and witnesses to family violence. *American Journal of Orthopsychiatry, 56,* 142-146.

James, B. (1989). *Treating traumatized children: New insights and creative interventions.* Lexington, MA: Lexington.

Johnson, R. J., & Montgomery, M. (1990). Children at multiple risk: Treatment and prevention. In R. T. Potter-Efron & P. S. Potter-Efron (Eds.), *Aggression, family violence, and chemical dependency* (pp. 145-163). New York: Haworth.

Jones, D. P. H., & McQuiston, M. G. (1989). *Interviewing the sexually abused child.* London, UK: Gaskell Royal College of Psychiatrists.

Jouriles, E. N., Murphy, C. M., & O'Leary, D. K. (1989). Interspousal aggression, marital discord, and child problems. *Journal of Consulting and Clinical Psychology, 57,* 453-455.

Kauffman, G. (1980). *Shame: The power of caring.* Cambridge, MA: Schenkman.

Kerouac, S., Taggart, M. E., Lescop, J., & Fortin, M. F. (1986). Dimensions of health in violent families. *Health Care for Women International, 7,* 413-426.

Kotlowitz, A. (1991). *There are no children here: The story of two boys growing up in the other America.* Garden City, NY: Doubleday.

Lansky, V. (1989). *Divorce book for parents: Helping your children cope with divorce and its aftermath.* New York: New American Library.

Larson, J., Anderson, J., & Morgan, A. (1984). *Effective stepparenting: Workshop models for family life education.* New York: Family Service America.

Layzer, J. I., Goodson, B. D., & Delange, C. (1986). Children in shelters. *Response to Victimization of Women and Children, 9*(2), 2-5.

Levine, M. B. (1975). Interpersonal violence and its effect on children: A study of 50 families in general practice. *Medicine, Science and Law, 15,* 172-176.

Lobel, K. (1986). *Naming the violence: Speaking out about lesbian battering.* Seattle: Seal Press.

Loseke, D. R. (1987). Lived realities and the construction of social problem: The case of wife abuse. *Symbolic Interaction, 10,* 224-243.

MacFarlane, K., & Waterman, J., with Conerly, S., Damon, L., Durfee, M., & Long, S. (1986). *Sexual abuse of young children.* New York: Guilford.

Martin, D. (1976). *Battered wives*. New York: Simon & Schuster.

Mathews, D. J. (1995). Parenting groups for men who batter. In E. Peled, P. G. Jaffe, & J. L. Edleson (Eds.), *Ending the cycle of violence: Community responses to children of battered women* (pp. 106-120). Thousand Oaks, CA: Sage.

Mathews, D. J., Matter, L., & Montgomery, M. (1990). *Wilder parenting manual*. Minneapolis: Wilder Foundation.

McNeill, M. (1987). Domestic violence: The skeleton in Tarasoff's closet. In D. J. Sonkin (Ed.), *Domestic violence on trial: Psychological and legal dimensions of family violence* (pp. 197-217). New York: Springer.

Miedzian, M. (1991). *Boys will be boys: Breaking the link between masculinity and violence*. Garden City, NY: Doubleday.

Moore, J. G. (1975). Yo-yo children: Victims of matrimonial violence. *Child Welfare, 54,* 557-566.

Nelson, B. J. (1984). *Making an issue of child abuse: Political agenda setting for social problems*. Chicago: University of Chicago Press.

Peled, E. (1993). *The experience of living with violence for preadolescent child witnesses of woman abuse*. Unpublished doctoral dissertation, University of Minnesota.

Peled, E., & Edleson, J. L. (1992). Multiple perspectives on groupwork with children of battered women. *Violence and Victims, 7,* 327-346.

Peled, E., Jaffe, P. J., & Edleson, J. (Eds.). (1995). *Ending the cycle of violence: Community response to children of battered women*. Thousand Oaks: Sage.

Pence, E., Hardesty, L., Steil, K., Soderberg, J., & Ottman, L. (1991). *What about the kids? Community intervention in domestic assault cases: A focus on children*. Duluth, MN: Duluth Domestic Abuse Intervention Project.

Pfouts, J. H., Schopler, J. H., & Hanley, H. C. (1981). Deviant behavior in child victims and bystanders in violent families. In R. J. Hunner & Y. E. Walker (Eds.), *Exploring the relationship between child abuse and delinquency* (pp. 79-99). New York: Allaheld, Osman.

Pleck, E. H. (1987). *Domestic tyranny: The making of a social policy against family violence from colonial times to present*. New York: Oxford University Press.

Pope, A., McHale, S., & Craighead, E. (1988). *Self-esteem enhancement in children and adolescents*. New York: Pergamon.

Quay, H. (1977). Measuring dimensions of deviant behavior: The Behavior Problem Checklist. *Journal of Abnormal Child Psychology, 5,* 277-289.

Ragg, D. M., & Webb, C. (1992). Group treatment for the preschool child witness of spouse abuse. *Journal of Child and Youth Care, 7,* 1-19.

Rosenbaum, A., & O'Leary, D. K. (1981). Children: The unintended victims of marital violence. *American Journal of Orthopsychiatry, 51,* 692-699.

Roy, M. (1988). *Children in the crossfire: Violence in the home—How does it affect our children?* Deerfield Beach, FL: Health Communications.

Salter, A. C. (1988). *Treating child sex offenders and victims: A practical guide*. Newbury Park, CA: Sage.

Saunders, D. G., & Azar, S. T. (1989). Treatment programs for family violence. In L. Ohlin & M. Tonry (Eds.), *Family violence* (pp. 481-546). Chicago: University of Chicago Press.

Silvern, L., & Kaersvang, L. (1989). The traumatized children of violent marriages. *Child Welfare, 68,* 421-436.

Silvern, L., Karyl, J., & Landis, T. Y. (1995). Individual psychotherapy for the traumatized children of abused women. In E. Peled, P. G. Jaffe, & J. L. Edleson (Eds.),

Ending the cycle of violence: Community responses to children of battered women (pp. 43-76). Thousand Oaks, CA: Sage.

Sonkin, D. J., Martin, D., & Walker, L. E. A. (1985). *The male batterer: A treatment approach.* New York: Springer.

Stacy, W., & Shupe, A. (1983). *The family secret: Domestic violence in America.* Boston: Beacon.

Stagg, V., Wills, G. D., & Howell, M. (1989). Psychopathology in early childhood witnesses of family violence. *Topics in Early Childhood Special Education, 9,* 73-87.

Straus, M. A. (1979). Measuring intrafamily conflict and violence: The Conflict Tactics Scale. *Journal of Marriage and the Family, 41,* 75-88.

Straus, M. A. (1991, September). *Children as witnesses to marital violence: A risk factor for lifelong problems among a nationally representative sample of American men and women.* Paper presented at the Ross Roundtable on "Children and Violence," Washington, DC.

Straus, M. A., & Gelles, R. J. (1986). Change in family violence from 1975-1985. *Journal of Marriage and the Family, 48,* 476-479.

Straus, M. A., Gelles, R. J., & Steinmetz, S. K. (1980). *Behind closed doors: Violence in the American Family.* Garden City, NY: Doubleday.

U.S. Bureau of the Census. (1990). *Household and family characteristics, March 1990 & 1989* (Current Population Report, Ser. P-20, No. 447:10). Washington, DC: Author.

Walker, L. E. (1979). *The battered woman.* New York: Harper & Row.

Wallerstein, J. S., & Kelly, J. B. (1980). *Surviving the breakup: How children and parents cope with divorce.* New York: Basic Books.

Westra, B., & Martin, H. P. (1981). Children of battered women. *Maternal Child Nursing Journal, 10,* 41-54.

Wilson, S. K., Cameron, S., Jaffe, P. G., & Wolfe, D. (1986). *Manual for a group program for children exposed to wife abuse.* London, Ontario: London Family Court Clinic.

Wolfe, D. A., Jaffe, P., Wilson, S. K., & Zak, L. (1985). Children of battered women: The relation of child behavior to family violence and maternal stress. *Journal of Consulting and Clinical Psychology, 53,* 657-665.

Wolfe, D. A., Jaffe, P., Wilson, S. K., & Zak, L. (1988). A multivariate investigation of children's adjustment to family violence. In G. T. Hotaling, D. Finkelhor, J. T. Kirkpatrick, & M. A. Straus (Eds.), *Family abuse and its consequences: New directions in research* (pp. 228-241). Newbury Park, CA: Sage.

Wolfe, D. A., Zak, L., Wilson, S., & Jaffe, P. (1986). Child witnesses to violence between parents: Critical issues in behavioral and social adjustment. *Journal of Abnormal Child Psychology, 14,* 95-104.

Yllö, K., & Bograd, M. (Eds.). (1988). *Feminist perspectives on wife abuse.* Newbury Park, CA: Sage.

Zimmerman, B. (1987). *Make beliefs.* New York: Juarionex.

Index

About the Authors

Einat Peled is a Lecturer in the Bob Shapell School of Social Work at Tel Aviv University, Israel, and was a Research Associate at the Domestic Abuse Project in Minneapolis at the time this manual was written. She has conducted research and published several articles on battered women and child witnesses of domestic violence, both in Israel and in the United States. She is a coeditor (with Peter Jaffe and Jeffrey Edleson) of *Ending the Cycle of Violence: Community Responses to Children of Battered Women* (Sage, 1995). She received her doctoral degree in social work from the University of Minnesota.

Diane Davis supervises the children's program at the Domestic Abuse Project. She is a licensed psychologist, a licensed graduate social worker, and is certified in Gestalt Therapy. She has also worked with children in both hospital and school settings and with adults in the areas of mental health and employee assistance. She received her master's degree in counseling psychology from St. Mary's College, Minnesota.